ASPECTS OF GÓNGORA'S *SOLEDADES*

PURDUE UNIVERSITY MONOGRAPHS IN ROMANCE LANGUAGES

Volume 1

John R. Beverley

Aspects of Góngora's "Soledades"

JOHN R. BEVERLEY

ASPECTS OF GÓNGORA'S "SOLEDADES"

AMSTERDAM / JOHN BENJAMINS B. V.

1980

ISBN 90 272 1711 4

For Gay

Contents

Preface

Góngora's *Soledades* have long been acknowledged as a classic of European poetry. Yet they remain today, nearly four centuries after their creation between 1613 and 1618, something of an enigma, something more referred to than read, a curious and slightly anachronistic monument to literary narcissism. Their influence proceeds like a subterranean river which at unexpected intervals breaks through to the surface: in Sor Juana and the Colonial Baroque, in Mallarmé, in Lorca and the Generation of '27, in the contemporary tragi-comic *soledades* of Lezama Lima, Carpentier, García Márquez, Juan Goytisolo. Today we are accustomed to regarding Góngora as a precursor of the "modern." But his poetry is rigorously constructed on the edifice of Greco-Latin literature and its derivations in the Western European Renaissance–a distillation of Classical tradition, but also that tradition rendered as a tomb, as something whose possibilities have been exhausted.

The immediate impact of the *Soledades* on the literary circles of the Court in the years following the appearance of manuscript copies of the *Soledad primera* in 1613 compelled a premature and, for the most part, sterile flowering of Spanish literary criticism. The poem became quickly ensnarled in a web of attacks and defenses, commentaries and allegorical exegeses. "Gongorism" prospered briefly in Spain, Portugal, and their colonies as a poetic manner to be imitated or condemned with equal facility and superficiality. The *reason* behind the manner–its force of human intelligence, its struggle with dissonance and contradiction–was lost sight of. Yet it is worth recalling Cervantes' admiration for Góngora's poetry. The *Soledades* appear around the same time as the second part of the *Quijote*, and they share with it the task of representing a social and historical reality which had suddenly, like their respective heroes, lost its way, become (in Gracián's phrase) a "mundo trabucado."

In part, what made the *Soledades* a necessary and privileged object of criticism–their sheer difficulty–was and remains a limitation to understanding the range of issues Góngora confronts in the poem. It is still current wisdom, for example, that they should properly be read and analyzed as an anthology of highly embellished lyric fragments loosely bound together as a celebration of the world of nature (but really a celebration of poetic technique *per se*).

Yet some of the Baroque commentaries on the poem speak of it as if it were a sort of novel in verse. There is a hero, a young man whom Góngora calls an "inconsiderado peregrino." We learn that he has been in a state of exile for "casi un lustro," that he is fleeing the presence of an "enemiga amada" (who is never specified), that he fears a "fin duro a mi destierro." He is shipwrecked and wanders on and around an unnamed shoreline for some five days. It is true that he acts mainly as a passive observer of the scenes and persons he encounters. But it is also clear that the unfolding of the poem is somehow built around his situation of loss, confusion, homelessness, desire. He is the *subject* of the intricate play of allusion, image, and syntax which composes the *Soledades* as a poetic language, a fact Góngora asks the reader to ponder in his opening proposition:

> Pasos de un peregrino son errante
> cuantos me dictó versos dulce musa:
> en soledad confusa
> perdidos unos, otros inspirados.

The present study of the *Soledades* is intended to summarize and discuss some of the problems which have seemed important to an understanding of them. Four issues that have been raised in recent work on the poem served as a starting point: (1) the implications of Góngora's own defense of his manner, the so-called "Carta en respuesta," as a poetics specific to the design and purpose of the *Soledades*; (2) the role of the pilgrim figure and the elements of a story and description built around him (in part, this involved my inclination, noted above, to read the *Soledades* as I would read a novel, as criticism has read the *Quijote*); (3) the related question of the elements which make up the "poetic unity" of the *Soledades* which the late R. O. Jones began to pose in his work on Góngora; (4) why, as many readers have noted, the second canto of the poem, the *Soledad segunda*, differs in mood, setting, and poetic decor from the first and why it is left apparently unfinished.

My concern with these issues betrayed a double impulse. Góngora criticism has tended to divide, broadly speaking, into two sometimes opposing camps: that of an analysis of *form*, concerned above all with the linguistic and prosodic problems posed by Góngora's art of verbal construction and exemplified by Dámaso Alonso's seminal *La lengua poética de Góngora* (Madrid: C.S.I.C., 1961), first published in 1935, and that of an analysis of *content*, concerned with the sedimentation in the poetry of Góngora's personal, historical, and ideological contingencies and exemplified by Robert Jammes's recent and encyclopedic *Etudes sur l'oeuvre poétique de Don Luis de Góngora* (Bordeaux: Féret et Fils, 1967). My own approach poses the need to integrate the methods and results of both camps, to find the ways in which they are complementary, the ways in which they correct each other's blind spots. My intention was not to annul previous interpretations, but to build on them, to show how they produce new combinations and hypotheses which can contribute to a better understanding of Góngora's very difficult achievement. I agree (but for different reasons) with the post-Tridentine detractors of the *Soledades* from Cascales to Menéndez y Pelayo that, in considering something like Góngora's poetry, aesthetic questions cannot be separated from ethical ones.

Jammes's *Etudes* had just arrived in America when I began my work on the *Soledades.* R. O. Jones directed me to them with the prudent counsel that what I was proposing to do had already been accomplished. I have no wish to detract from the value of such a painstaking work. The *Etudes* are, I believe, the most significant critical revision of Góngora and his age that has appeared since the work of the Generation of '27. But Jammes did not answer the questions I had about the *Soledades*, those that I have noted above. Moreover, it seemed to me that in his discussion of the *Soledades* he was coming close to reviving the old and discredited notion of "two Góngoras"–angel of light / angel of darkness– in a new form. One of the basic premises of the *Etudes* is that Góngora shows contradictory practices as an artist. On the one hand, he acts essentially as a flatterer, seeking through his poetry to ingratiate himself with the ruling circles of the aristocracy; on the other hand, he acts as a critic of the dominant values and perceptions of his society, disdaining the temptations of the Court and seeking consolation from the confusion and crisis of Spain's imperial policy in nostalgic and elegant linguistic utopias of his own making. Jammes is correct to give emphasis to this dichotomy, but it unfortunately leads him into what I consider the cardinal error of judging the *Soledad primera* as representing the "authentic" (or critical-utopian) dimension of Góngora's art and dismissing the *Soledad segunda* as a sycophantic pastiche disfigured by "dissonances." For example: ". . . je suppose qu'une fois terminée la *Soledad primera* . . . il restait à Góngora un certain nombre d'ébauches, de projets, ou, comme disent les peintres, d'*études* qui n'avaient pas eu leur place dans le poème achevé dont elles auraient dérangé l'harmonie." Or: ". . . il [Góngora] abandonne le thème du mépris de Cour et, de la façon la plus inattendue, il transforme la seconde *Solitude* en éloge du compte de Niebla, c'est-à-dire en poème courtisan." While I think every reader of the poem will agree that the *Soledad segunda* is more "dissonant" than the first, the question would seem to be, especially with such an intimate work as the *Soledades*, why this is the case, rather than whether the "good" or the "bad" Góngora is writing.

. . .

Góngora's poems and letters, other than the *Soledades*, are cited in this work from the versions provided in the *Obras completas* edited by Juan and Isabel Millé y Giménez, specifically the fourth edition (Madrid: Aguilar, 1956), and are identified by the number assigned them there. For example, the sonnet of *circa* 1594, "Cosas, Celalba mía, he visto extrañas," would be noted as Millé 261, Góngora's "Carta en respuesta" as Millé, Epistolario 2. I have used as a working text of the *Soledades* Dámaso Alonso's 1927 version in an edition published by Ediciones del Arbol (Madrid, 1935). This has the advantage of offering a better numeration of the verses and the, in some cases extensive, textual variants contained in the early manuscript copies and printed editions of the poem. (In his lifetime Góngora permitted only manuscript copies of the *Soledades* to circulate, and these were subject to corrections by Góngora himself and emendations by unauthorized copyists.) Alonso's 1927 version of the text has been the basis for most modern editions of the *Soledades*. (I have noted some of the reservations that have been expressed, principally by Maurice Molho, about Alonso's "paragraphing" of the text at the beginning of Chapter 3 and have been working on a new version of the poem which is scheduled to be published in Editorial Cátedra's classics series.) The reader whose principal language, like mine, is English will want to consult the translations of G. F. Cunningham (Baltimore: Johns Hopkins University Press, 1968) and E. M. Wilson (Cambridge: The University Press, 1965). Pellicer's *Lecciones solemnes a las obras de Don Luis de Góngora* (Madrid, 1630) have been brought out in facsimile in the Textos y estudios clásicos de las literaturas hispánicas series published by Georg Olms Verlag (Hildesheim and New York, 1971). His remarks on the *Soledades* are often quite insightful, often absurdly pedantic. The other major Baroque commentary on the poem is Salcedo Coronel's *"Soledades" comentadas* (Madrid, 1636). Dámaso Alonso's version in prose, contained in most reeditions of his 1927 text, is also a great help to the reader. I have indicated the location of passages from the *Soledades* in this monograph when necessary by verse number and an abbreviation of the canto in which they appear. (Because E. M. Wilson's bilingual edition uses a passage that is not included in the standard version of the *Soledades*, his numeration of the *Soledad primera* does not correspond with that of the Alonso text.) In order to make my commentary on specific passages from the *Soledades* more immediately understandable, I have italicized certain words or syntactical units. I have taken this liberty in my rendition of more than thirty passages, and it would be tedious to the reader were I to indicate each time that the italics have been added. The reader should bear in mind, then, that where in this monograph italics occur in a passage from the *Soledades*, they have been added by myself.

The following abbreviations appear in the notes:

B.A.E.	Biblioteca de Autores Españoles
BHS	*Bulletin of Hispanic Studies*
C.S.I.C.	Consejo Superior de Investigaciónes Científicas
MLN	*Modern Language Notes*

RFE	*Revista de Filología Española*
RFH	*Revista de Filología Hispánica*

In somewhat different versions, Chapters 2, 3, and 6 of this study have appeared in, respectively, *Modern Language Notes*, 88 (1973), *Dispositio*, 3, No. 9 (1978), and *Ideologies and Literature*, 1, No. 5 (1978).

. . .

No one can begin to try to understand Góngora's poetry without becoming a part of a critical enterprise shared by many people in different centuries and countries. As Lorca noted, "A Góngora no hay que leerlo sino estudiarlo." My first acknowledgement, then, is to those who have shared this difficult but pleasant labor with me. Ira Wade and Américo Castro at Princeton taught me to understand that the closed space of a literary text was at once an integral part and a reflection of the ways peoples and nations make history. Joaquín Casalduero inadvertently fathered my interest in the *Soledades* by suggesting one day that I study Valle-Inclán's aesthetics. This led "by a *commodius victus* of circuitous intent" back to Góngora. But I owe him much more than this, as he knows. The eclecticism and excitement of the early years of the Department of Literature at the University of California, San Diego were important factors in shaping the design and concerns of the present study, which was begun as a doctoral dissertation there. I am grateful, in particular, for the lessons of Herbert Marcuse and Fred Jameson, for the example of Carlos Blanco-Aguinaga, and for the long discussions on politics, poetry, and philosophy with my friend Claude Dupuydenus. Claudio Guillén nursed my interest in the *Soledades* through a long period of indecision. He had the prudence of Gracián's *discreto* to let me find my own way, to be both absent and present in the results. Harriet Frey pruned and corrected the initial manuscript with the sure instinct of a classicist. Donald Coleman, Juan Goytisolo, Thomas Hart, and, especially, Elias Rivers gave me in different ways and at different moments the insight and encouragement I needed to continue my work. The Department of Spanish and Portuguese at the University of Minnesota allowed me to test my ideas on Góngora with a group of very bright and demanding students. William Whitby and his colleagues in the Purdue University Monographs series were both rigorous and kind. Their suggestions enabled me to produce a much finer manuscript than the one I submitted to them. My wife Gay has had her own work to develop, but I owe her the greatest debt for the years we have spent together.

Introduction

It was no accident that Dámaso Alonso found it necessary to incorporate in his work on Góngora's poetic language some of the concepts of Saussure's structural linguistics. The nature of any linguistic sign, Saussure had suggested, proposed a relation between two *relata*: signifier and signified, speaker and hearer, intention and understanding, language rule and language use, convention and invention. The attack on the *Soledades* in the early seventeenth century was directed against Góngora's deviations from what were regarded as the permissible norms of poetic communication. It maintained that in the *Soledades* language, in effect, had ceased to signify, that Góngora in wanting to create a utopia of language had fallen instead into the sin of Babel. Recently, in an aphorism bearing on what I take to be the formalist canon on the *Soledades*, Maurice Molho has remarked: "Il convient donc de lire les *Solitudes* comme un essai de reconstruction du langage–d'un langage–à partir du langage, et des rapports sur lesquels il se fond."[1]

But the problem of the creation of language in the *Soledades* is not something peculiar to language alone. Linguistic formalism can tell us a great deal about the poem, show its precise mechanisms of imagination and construction. It leaves, however, a number of questions "in parenthesis": Why this particular act of linguistic invention? What is its relation to the historical time and space in which it signifies? Why the enormous effort and dangers it involves? Why the central figure of the pilgrim? Why his restlessness, his failure to find consolation? Góngora's language, like any language, is an act of communication that implies the social urgency of a message that must be communicated. To borrow Saussure's metaphors, the *Soledades* compose not only a *langue*, as if their purpose was to be an autonomous and self-referential formal system, but also a *parole*, a way of being and acting in the social and historical world that circumscribes Góngora's practice as a poet.

One should find it strange that a work which is supposed to be an absolute poetry–a "territory" of language accessible only to an aristocracy of aesthetes–displays such a detailed and reiterated interest in the ways ordinary people make their living. Let me note only two of many examples in the *Soledades*. The goatherds who shelter the pilgrim after the shipwreck offer him a cup of milk:

y en boj, aunque rebelde, a quien el torno
forma elegante dió sin culto adorno,
leche que exprimir vió la Alba aquel día
–mientras perdían con ella
los blancos lilios de su frente bella–,
gruesa le dan y fría,
impenetrable casi a la cuchara,
del viejo Alcimedón invención rara. (I, 145-52)

Some days later the pilgrim comes upon a party of fishermen who invite him to join them as they cast their nets:

Dando el huésped licencia para ello,
recurren no a las redes que, mayores,
mucho Océano y pocas aguas prenden,
sino a las que ambiciosas menos penden,
laberinto nudoso de marino
Dédalo, si de leño no, de lino,
fábrica escrupulosa, y aunque incierta,
siempre murada, pero siempre abierta. (II, 73-80)

The simple curve of a wooden cup turned on a lathe, the "invención rara" of a spoon, the freshness and thickness of curded milk, the different sizes and weaves of the nets are observed here with an obvious attention to forms of elaboration and use. This is hardly a language which "alludes" to reality only to escape it in spirals of embellishment. It rejects the merely "decorative" ("forma elegante . . . sin culto adorno") and the pretentious ("redes que . . . mucho Océano y pocas aguas prenden"). It seems more a language whose own concern with technique is bound up in the qualities of the simple objects of labor or consumption it is describing, objects which, like Góngora's images, are devices for *capturing* and *containing.*

If the *Soledades* are an anthology of lyrical descriptions and episodes, what binds these together is that they serve to index a group of social forms which correspond to the technologies portrayed in passages such as the two above.[2] The poem presents at least four different types of human community: an Arcadian society of goatherds and hunters living in the mountains; a country village, apparently the center of a region of cultivated fields, where the pilgrim is a guest at a wedding; a coastal island inhabited by a single family who depends economically on fishing, artisanry, and garden farming; a feudal estate and its castle which form the background to a description of a hawking expedition. An epic narrative interpolated in the *Soledad primera* by an old shepherd recounts the discovery and conquest of Spain's overseas empire in the sixteenth century and pictures the enterprise as a misfortune, an act of tragic vanity. (R. O. Jones once described the *Soledades* as "anti-imperialist pastoral.")[3] Throughout the poem there are notes on the contemporary life of the Court and the great cities which serve as a counterpoint to the pastoral landscapes and rustic huts the pilgrim passes through. The pilgrim himself is someone who has lost touch with his own society, an exile sometimes consumed by nostalgia, sometimes hoping to find in his journey a new homeland. The places he encounters in the *Soledades* confront him with images of *natural* economies and societies where men and women live in close intimacy with manual labor and with the variety of nature, where production is for use rather than personal profit, where equality and generosity still reign.

Who is this pilgrim? In part, of course, Góngora; in part, the reader who is "addressed" by the poem. Christopher Caudwell described the English poets who were Góngora's near contemporaries as "shy, proud men writing alone in their studies–appealing from court life to the country or heaven":

> Poetry, drawing away from the collective life of the court, can only withdraw into the privacy of the bourgeois study, austerely furnished, shared only with a few chosen friends, surroundings so different from the sleeping and waking publicity of court life that it rapidly revolutionises poetic technique. . . . Language reflects the change. Lyrics no longer become something that a gentleman could sing to his lady; conceits are no longer something which could be tossed in courtly conversation. Poetry is no longer something to be roared out to a mixed audience. It smells of the library where it was produced. It is a learned man's poetry: student's poetry. Poetry is read, not declaimed: it is correspondingly subtle and intricate.[4]

With due allowance, this can stand also as a portrait of the *Soledades* and their author. Góngora, as Robert Jammes has shown, belonged to the lower orders of the Andalusian provincial aristocracy, orders which had not fared well under the economic changes and inflation imposed by Hapsburg centralism and imperialism. This implied two things: the poet's lack of extensive property in land or other forms of nobiliary wealth like the *censos* or *juros* issued by the Court against its income from the colonies, and a special love for and knowledge of his native region combined with a barely concealed distaste for Madrid and the intrigue of power and money-making.[5] Like so many other titled but impecunious *letrados* in the Golden Age period, he will have to seek a position in the state and ecclesiastical apparatus erected by Hapsburg absolutism and the Spanish Counter Reformation. After his studies at Salamanca, he is awarded a prebend at the Cathedral of Córdoba which provides him with a meager income. But there is little in his life or work which suggests anything more than the most nominal attachment to the Church, and his heterodox tastes and pursuits place him more than once in conflict with his superiors. His real ambition is to gain fame and influence through his poetry. He begins his literary career as an apprentice of Herrera's Sevillian school; around 1585, when he is barely into his twenties, he seems, however, to have achieved his own style and following. His poetry and friends, which include some important figures in the Hapsburg ministries like the Count of Villamediana, allow him to try his hand at intervals as one of the hundreds of talented petty *hidalgos* jockeying for recognition and reward in a court which, after Philip II's death in 1598, is less and less able to oblige them. (In this, he shares the frustrations and financial difficulties Cervantes experienced after his return from captivity in Algeria.) In 1609 he finds himself in a legal tangle in Madrid, the victim, apparently, of his own indiscretions at the Court and the growing animosity of literary rivals like Quevedo and Lope. Between 1610 and 1618 he lives in a sort of semi-exile from Madrid in a small country estate near Córdoba, the Huerta de Marcos. Here he dedicates himself to the creation of the *Polifemo* and the two cantos of the *Soledades*. The Andalusian countryside shapes the form and theme of these poems; they reflect a disenchantment with the Court and the political destiny of Spain, a desire to construct something that can be posed against an oppressive authority. On his departure from Madrid, he writes this ironic valedictory:

Dichoso el que pacífico se esconde
a este civil rüido, y litigante,
o se concierta o por poder responde,

sólo por no ser miembro corteggiante
de sierpe prodigiosa, que camina
la cola, como el gámbaro, delante.

¡Oh Soledad, de la quietud divina
dulce prenda, aunque muda, ciudadana
del campo, y de sus Ecos convecina! (Millé 395)

But the temptation of the Court is always with him, and the poems of his rural "soledad" are also shaped by its tensions and promises. In 1618 Góngora returns to Madrid, seduced by the offer of a position as chaplain to the royal family. He seems at the height of his fortune and artistic powers, only to find himself suddenly caught up along with his friends and patrons in the precipitous collapse of the Duke of Lerma's ministry and the rise of the new favorite, Olivares. He spends the remaining decade of his life struggling against debt, the animosity of his many enemies and rivals, and his own failing health and sanity. In 1627 he dies in Córdoba; in the same year, the Inquisition prohibits the sale of the first public edition of his poetry, Juan de Vicuña's *Obras en verso del Homero español*.

Regarding this trajectory, Jammes observes: "On peut dire que la carrière de Góngora est exemplaire, car elle suit la même courbe descendante que l'ensemble de la monarchie espagnole durant la même periode."[6] In the eyes of the *arbitristas* whose company and advice Góngora valued, the Spain of Lerma and Philip III is a nation undergoing a general crisis, deluded by the glitter of precious metals and a false dream of imperial grandeur and aristocratic sublimation. González de Cellorigo suggested the Cervantine image of "una república de hombres encantados, que [viven] fuera del orden natural."[7] The vast empire so quickly and confidently gained begins to acquire the aspect of a labyrinth or ruin. The great Indian civilizations of America lie in rubble; the population which survives the Conquest is reduced to the servitude of forced labor in the mines or the *encomiendas* of the colonial elite. The exhaustion of the gold and silver lodes, the depopulation of both America and parts of Castile, the fiscal crisis of the state and the domestic economy assume alarming proportions in the years following the death of Philip II.[8]

Góngora reflects the crisis of the empire in his own vision of the New World:

> ara del Sol edades ciento, ahora
> templo de quien el Sol aun no es estrella,
> la grande América es, oro sus venas,
> sus huesos plata, que dichosamente,
> si ligurina dió marinería
> a España en uno y otro alado pino,
> interés ligurino
> su rubia sangre hoy día,
> su medula chupando está luciente. (Millé 404)

The "ligurina marinería" refers to Columbus and the Discovery; the "interés ligurino" to the profits of the Genoese banks on the loans they extended to the Hapsburgs: America, given to Spain "dichosamente," is a sacral body now bled to death by greed and exploitation. (The phrase "ara del Sol edades ciento" may be read as either "ara de cien edades del Sol" or "de cien Soledades"– in both cases, that is, as a *utopian* space.) The gold and silver extracted at such enormous human cost from the American mines pass into Spain, consolidating the power of a leisured aristocracy and church, creating new cities like Madrid whose sole function is to house and service a huge state and ecclesiastical bureaucracy. The policies of the Hapsburgs leave a heritage of economic and political repression (the defeat of the Comunero revolts); excessive taxation of the productive sectors of the Spanish economy (the aristocracy remains exempt from this obligation); increasing national debt; unproductive investment in government *censos* and *juros*, military and luxury goods, or gifts to the church; periodic fiscal crises; and rapid inflation. What Vicens Vives called the Castilian "bourgeois meteor"–the rise of a prosperous manufacturing and trading bourgeoisie in the late fifteenth and early sixteenth centuries–burns out. Much of the American gold and silver finds its way out of Spain to the banks of Amsterdam and Genoa, to the merchant and manufacturing ports of England, northern France, and the Hanseatic League. There it stimulates the newly emerging capitalist franchise. As the flow of precious metals to Spain declines towards the end of the sixteenth century, the country discovers it has nothing to put in its place. In the decades following the defeat of the Armada, Spain's military and naval hegemony fades as the other emerging nation states of Europe and the Ottoman Empire step forward to compete for colonies, trade routes, and subject populations. The empire begins the process of contraction which will culminate in 1898. The Netherlands continue to press their century-long war of national liberation, posing the bourgeois ideal of a free merchant republic against the feudal absolutism of the Hapsburgs. It is a war that Spain cannot win, but cannot seem to lose decisively either. Beyond it, with the rise of Olivares' ministry, lie the further depredations of the Thirty Years' War. By 1640, the regions of Hapsburg Spain itself–Catalonia, Andalusia, Portugal–attempt to break away from the weakened Castilian center. Portugal succeeds in freeing itself; the other regions are crushed. Spain remains a power, but only at the cost of subjecting its own population and resources to strains and sacrifices that will severely retard its possibilities for growth. The social classes which form the backbone of the Puritan revolution in England–the manufacturing bourgeoisie, the peasants and small landowning gentry of the *municipios*, the artisans and the members of the professions–are the sections of the population most damaged by the emerging crisis. The masses–the urban Lazarillos of the picaresque novel and the peasants of the *comedias* and *entremeses*–find their conditions of life deteriorating. The rise of the cities in the sixteenth century dislocates the traditional patterns of life and production in the countryside; a "marginal" population appears, living off petty crime, beggary, odd jobs, fraud: the floating world of Quevedo's *Buscón*. Unemployment, corruption, the cult of appearances, and bureaucracy are rife. Lope notes cynically:

> Todos andan bien vestidos
> y quéjanse de los precios,
> de medio arriba, romanos,
> de medio abajo, romeros.

In this setting, schizophrenia seems to be a prerequisite of enlightenment: Cervantes' Vidriera and Quijote, Quevedo's *Sueños*, Góngora's "soledad confusa." The sturdy humanism of the early sixteenth century has yielded to a "national" culture characterized by conformism, chauvinism, and religious and intellectual pedantry. The Court, dominated by the conflicting parties of the great nobility and by a spirit of petty Machiavellianism, is incapable of staking the country to policies that might begin to reverse the decline and restore the freedom and well-being of the people. To deflect popular discontent, it contrives acts of ill-considered opportunism like the expulsion of the Moriscos of Andalusia and Valencia in 1610. The capacity to think through the problems of the country has not been lost; if anything the critiques and reform projects of the *arbitristas* like González de Cellorigo show an unexpected economic sophistication and realism. But the capacity to act on these suggestions seems paralyzed, perhaps because they threaten to undermine the power and privileges of the aristocracy. L. J. Woodward has noted Góngora's close friendship with Pedro de Valencia, a utopian humanist in the tradition of Thomas More and his Erasmist colleagues in Italy, Spain, and the Netherlands. Valencia served as a sort of editor of the *Soledades*, and what survives of his correspondence with Góngora shows him as a refined literary connoisseur and a rigorous critic of errors of taste in the poem. But he is also someone who, as Woodward explains, "advocated the break-up of the large estates and their distribution among the peasants, the construction of an economy based on service and as far as possible free from the evils of money and credit." He shares with Góngora that respect, curious in two men who are both *letrados* and aristocrats, for the processes of manual labor we have observed in several images of the *Soledades*. For Valencia, ". . . the rich are objects of contempt, the manual laborers, especially those who work on the land, are properly the masters of society."[9]

The *Soledades*, I want to argue, are as much a way of posing the problems of Spain's crisis in the early seventeenth century as the work of the *arbitristas*. To pose these problems correctly, to show that there may be alternatives still present in the life of the country, to reeducate himself and his readers, the poet has to escape from their immediate pressure to "another world." The retreat into art is a pilgrimage: the search for the image and quality of a possible utopia that can be placed against the experience of history as disaster, blind fate. Góngora's poetic manner represents the transfer to aesthetics of questions of social ethics and political economy that cannot be "thought" in their own languages. The retreat should come back into time in the form of a plausible *redemption*. But it does not. The *Soledades* end with an image of uncertainty and horror: "y a la estigia deidad con bella esposa." This is what makes Góngora and his art finally different from Caudwell's account of the Puritan poets. These address a class which, in the seventeenth century, is beginning to exercise its ideas and institutions with increasing authority. Their poetry reflects and in turn helps to form the values and aspirations of the class, its images of community and history, its morality and personal style, its sense of revolutionary legitimacy. Beyond their withdrawal to the scholar's study and their attacks on the vanity of the Court, they are able to intuit the advent of a "new Jerusalem," and they bend their art and their lives to serve its birth.

Góngora has neither this confidence nor this possibility. The crisis of Hapsburg absolutism is a sterile one. Pierre Vilar has summarized it best: "El imperialismo español ha sido en realidad 'la etapa suprema' de la sociedad que él mismo ha contribuido a destruir. Pero en su propio solar, en Castilla y hacia 1600, *el feudalismo entra en agonía sin que exista nada a punto para reemplazarle*."[10] The *Soledades* are an attempt to understand and humanize the force of history in a society history has turned against. They are directed not to an emerging class which has, or is in the process of developing, the power to effect a reconstruction of the social order, but rather to a diminishing elite capable of understanding Góngora's inventions and intimations. These readers are, like the poet himself, isolated and contradictory figures, aristocratic radicals who sometimes challenge, sometimes celebrate the authority of the social class that nurtures them. To the extent that they understand what has to be done, they are powerless to act on that understanding, compelled to hold it as a secret shared in conversations, allusions, letters. Lucidity—the "claridad" Dámaso Alonso found in the *Soledades*—yields not a new ethics but instead aestheticism and a private ideology of stoic tacitism.

The *Soledades* are both a reflection and a symptom of the Spanish Decadence. In this sense they are a failure, something that falls short of its promise, that has to be abandoned to a disillusion Góngora felt more intimately than we can understand. What is lasting in them, however, and what allows them to be recommenced is his willingness to embrace and express the deepest contradictions in himself and the concrete moment of history in which he lives and works. The loneliness of this task—the construction of solitude—conceals a communion with other human beings and other possibilities of life and art which extend beyond this moment and its terrible knot of determinations.

PART I

Towards a Poetics of the "Soledades"

There is always a dialectical relationship–what Piaget called a "return bounce"–between the activity of study and research and the object that the scholar began by examining.

Lucien Goldmann

1

Góngora's "Carta en respuesta"

Francisco Cascales, the typical humanist of the literary Counter Reformation in Spain, commented on his reading of an early text of the *Soledades*:

> ¡Oh diabólico poema! Pues ¿qué ha pretendido nuestro poeta? Yo lo diré; destruir la poesía. . . . ¿En qué manera? Volviendo a su primer caos las cosas; haciendo que ni los pensamientos se entiendan, ni las palabras se conozcan con la confusión y desorden.[1]

The *Cartas filológicas* dealing with Góngora and the *Soledades* suggest again and again that the poem and the positions taken by its defenders imply a kind of *atheism* in questions of poetics. (Three centuries later Vicente Gaos writes: "La poesía de Góngora es constitutivamente atea, en efecto.")[2] The *Soledades* are a Babel, the delirium of a language which seeks to function independent of religious doctrine and pedagogy, which is motivated only by the vanity of its creator. Góngora's celebrated enigmas uncover no principle of truth, no mysteries of nature, religion, or morality, only an artificial riddling and unriddling of puns, allusions, images, and tricks of syntax: "son indisolubles, inútiles y nugatorias, que sólo sirven de dar garrote al entendimiento." To Cascales, therefore, the Góngora of the *Soledades* is a "Mahoma de la poesía española."

What is evident here is that the debate over the *Soledades* in the literary circles of the Court of Philip III quickly escalated beyond questions of literary taste and decorum. The suggestion of the heretical status of Góngora's new manner (compare Quevedo's "Yo te untaré mis versos con tocino") meant not so much that the "Microcósmote Dios de inquiridones" was actually a *converso*. (Robert Jammes has laid this much-debated issue to rest.)[3] Rather it was more a charge that Góngora's way of doing poetry departed from the canons of the prevailing poetics in which questions of this kind would have to be posed.

Cascales' remarks posit themselves along the thin and increasingly strained line that separated the rhetorics and literary theory of the Spanish Counter Reformation from the actual *practice* of the poets and writers. (One sign of this separation between theory and practice is the appearance in the early seventeenth century of statements on poetics by the writers themselves: Lope's *Arte nuevo de hacer comedias*, Carrillo y Sotomayor's *Libro de la erudición poética*, Cervantes at intervals in the *Quijote*, Tirso in *Los cigarrales de Toledo*, etc.) Andrée Collard has recently argued that in Góngora's major poetry of the *Soledades* period (roughly 1610 to 1621) the didactic concept of the poet as *vates* or prophet crucial to a pedagogic poetics is abandoned in favor of a "hedonistic" concept of the poet as pure artificer derived from the exercises of literary connoisseurship. "En realidad," she writes, "Góngora inventa un nuevo género poético en que la 'utilidad' desaparece frente al arte descriptivo. . . . Reúne rasgos de la poesía tradicional épica, lírica y dramática, quitándoles su antigua función."[4] The point is to agree in a certain sense with Cascales and the denigrators of Góngora who come to be known as the *detractores* that the *Soledades* are heretical, that they no longer belong in the context of a religio-moral determination of subjects and forms of imitation. Where for Cascales the poem and not the integrity of the normative poetics must therefore be condemned to non-sense, the revision of Góngora in the twentieth century has tended, inversely, to a celebration of poetic *formalism*. For the Alonso of the seminal "Claridad y belleza de las *Soledades*" (1927), the value of Gongorism was predicated on a sense of the crisis of the realist novel and the new attention (Cubism) to a "puro placer de formas": "Contra el interés novelesco, el estético. En lugar del interés novelesco—alimento de las actividades espirituales de orden práctico—la densa polimorfía de temas de belleza."[5] The source to which the poet-Gongorists of the Generation of '27 referred was the *Apologético en favor de Don Luis de Góngora* by the Peruvian humanist Juan de Espinosa Medrano, a work which dismissed the "doctrinal" objections of Cascales and the traditionalist school as irrelevant to the specific nature of poetic creation and enjoyment.[6]

These definitions are not without their point; formalist poetics, both in the seventeenth century and in our own, have served to rescue Góngora's major works, especially the *Soledades*, from the oblivion to which they have been repeatedly condemned. Collard's notion of the poet-artificer, in particular, touches on the common theme of Góngora's defenders in the Madrid Court who were given to opposing an aristocracy of aesthetes versed in subtleties of poetic theme and technique, to the pedants and "vulgarizers" of didactic poetics. There is a problem, however. Góngora, in his own defense of the *Soledades*, the "Carta en respuesta de la que le escribieron" (Millé, Epistolario 2), rather explicitly activates the traditional poet-*vates topos*. "Pregunto yo," he asks at the beginning of his reply to the charges made against his poem, "¿han sido útiles al mundo las poesías y aun las profecías (que vates se llama el profeta como el poeta)? Sería error negarlo." If we accept Collard's definition (which summarizes a formalist poetics of the *Soledades*), Góngora's language here has to seem paradoxical.

The "Carta en respuesta" was addressed by the poet in his semi-exile in Córdoba as an open letter meant to accompany the manuscript copies of the *Soledades* which were being distributed in Madrid by his friend Mendoza. It responds to an earlier "Carta de un amigo de Don Luis de Góngora que le escribió acerca de sus *Soledades*" (Millé, Epistolario 127), possibly by Lope and/or his literary cohorts. The "Carta de un amigo," as it has come to be known, is the opening move in the long and complicated debate over the *Soledades* that was to occupy Spanish writers and critics on both sides for the next ten years.[7] It sketches the image which was to become the common currency of the *detractores*: "muchos se han persuadido que le alcanzó algún ramalazo de la desdicha de Babel." If it was Góngora's intention, the anonymous writer continues, to merit a special achievement for being "inventor de dificultar la construcción de el romance," he should in the *Soledades*, if they are indeed his at all, recognize a cardinal error. "Mostrar agudeza" is one thing, but the consequent production must attend to the Horatian norm of the useful "wrapped in" the pleasing; the *Soledades* ignore this in favor of verbal fireworks. The letter ends with the demand "y pues las invenciones en tanto son buenas en cuanto tienen de útil, honroso y deleitable, lo que basta para quedar constituidas en razón de bien, dígame V.m. si hay algo en esta su novedad. . . ."

Góngora, in recovering the sense of the poet-*vates* concept in his "Carta en respuesta," intends to meet this demand head-on. He pushes away with ironic ingenuity the charge of creating a Babel:

> Al ramalazo de la desdicha de Babel, aunque el símil es humilde, quiero descubrir un secreto no entendido de V.m. al escribirme. No los confundió Dios a ellos con darles lenguaje confuso, sino en el mismo ellos se confundieron, tomando piedra por agua, y agua por piedra. . . . Yo no envió confusas las *Soledades*, sino la malicia de las voluntades en su mismo lenguaje halla confusión por parte del sujeto inficionado con ellas.

The *Soledades* are to be considered useful in the same sense as the intricate obscurity of Ovid in the *Metamorphoses*; the difficulty of language and conceit is meant to construct the poem as an *exercise* which the reader must work his way through in order to arrive at a keener faculty of mind. (And not of mere wit: "digo a V.m. que ya mi edad más está para veras que para burlas.") Góngora poses in relation to the poet-*vates* concept an image of allegorical and eschatological exegesis: the surface of the text as a shell or "corteza" which contains a hidden kernel of meaning:

> . . . da causa a que, vacilando el entendimiento en fuerza del discurso, trabajándole (pues crece con cualquier acto de valor) alcance lo que así en la lectura superficial de sus versos no pudo entender; luego hase de confesar que tiene utilidad avivar el ingenio, y eso nació de la obscuridad del poeta. Eso mismo hallará V.m. en mis *Soledades*, si tiene capacidad para quitar la corteza y descubrir lo misterioso que encubren.

Orozco Díaz explains that "la duplicidad de valores, de esa *corteza*, o sea de complicados planos verbales de figuras, y de ese sentido oculto o *misterioso*, supone algo caracterı̆stico de la obra barroca, que procura, de una parte, actuar sensorialmente deslumbrando con luces, colores y sonidos, y después nos inquieta en busca de un fondo o sentido oculto."[8] But what is the nature of this hidden sense?

Serrano de Paz, around 1636 in his *Comentarios* on the *Soledades*, represents one rather bizarre consequence of Góngora's apparent invitation to a hermeneutic reading. As Dámaso Alonso pointed out, the *Comentarios* were meant to rival the canonic exegeses of Pellicer and Salcedo Coronel. Where these had unriddled the *Soledades* line by line in the manner of Herrera's studies of Garcilaso, Serrano de Paz wanted to show that the poem was a systematic allegory on the order of Dante's *Divine Comedy*, even at the cost of inventing meanings which Góngora himself might not have intended:

> . . . nunca entendí que el intento del Poema se acortasse en lo literal solo, antes siempre juzgué que el Poeta escondió otro sentido mayor del que muestra la letra, y assí fui discurriendo las alegorías que en el propósito se podían dar. Y no quiero que crea alguno que doy éstas por las intencionadas del Poeta, que acaso escondió otras muy diversas, pero en cosa tan oculta valga a cada uno su juyzio.

The results of this enterprise (for example, an interpretation of the fishing scenes of the second *Soledad* as, detail by detail, an allegory of the search for knowledge) Alonso properly makes fun of.[9] But the *Comentarios* suggest, on the other hand, the kind of *reading* of the *Soledades* Sor Juana might have done in preparation for her *Primero Sueño*. They illustrate too that the defense of the *Soledades* in the Baroque period was not made solely on the grounds of the legitimacy of a formalist poetics, that in Calderón and Gracián, for example, elements of Góngora's style and imagery would be drawn into the service of precisely that which Cascales thought they offended, Catholic pedagogic allegory.

More conventionally, Góngora's "misterioso" has been taken as referring to the presence in the poem of the theme of "menosprecio de corte, alabanza de aldea" so dear to the poets of the Renaissance. In the early commentaries, like Pellicer's, this was joined with a sense that Góngora had intended his poem in its finished state as a narrative in four cantos or *soledades* of the stations of an aristocratic disillusion with life which would culminate in a hermitage or solitude of the desert. The late R. O. Jones, basing himself also on this point in the "Carta en respuesta," undertook to explain the poem as a Neoplatonic gnostic allegory, a kind of Spanish and Baroque reworking of the *Enneads*. He read the *Soledades* as a philosophical pastoral which furnished around the narrative device of the pilgrim a series of didactic emblems of natural and cosmological harmony and providence. These emblems operate to organize the cornucopia of scenes and impressions that appear in tumultous and often contradictory profusion in the surface of the poem's language. Their compositional model was to be found, according to Jones, in Neoplatonic musical theory, specifically the idea of reality as a *musica mundana*, a world of order and stability behind the texture of sensory appearances. "Embodied in the proliferating images of life and beauty in the *Soledades*," he concluded, "is a theme which is nothing less majestic than the principles on which, for Góngora, the world is founded."[10]

I will have occasion to return many times in the course of this study to the issues raised by Jones. For the moment, however, let me simply note that what Jones saw as a hidden *content* in the poem is also a feature of its *form*, of its texture of language and meter. What I want to develop here is a sense in which the achievements of a formalist analysis, like Dámaso Alonso's "Función estructural de las pluralidades," and a hermeneutic or thematic study must be brought into relation. Consider a perhaps intentional ambiguity in the passage from the "Carta en respuesta" we have been dealing with. Góngora claimed that the usefulness of his manner consisted in its being an exercise of wit. But an exercise to what end? Serrano de Paz's allegorical kernel, Jones's Neoplatonic gnosis? In part yes. But the language of the passage also indicates that this exercise would be somehow valuable in itself as a form of mental recreation required by the difficulty of the writing. Góngora's formula "trabajar el discurso" seems to equate the poet's labor in composing the "tropos" and the reader's in deciphering them. It is an invitation to have the reader "complete" a text which Góngora will leave (at the end of the *Soledad segunda*) strategically incomplete.

Góngora is close to the idea of *difficoltà* which had been advanced earlier in the aesthetic theory of the Mannerists as a justification for their tendencies towards formal and thematic hypercomplication. They held that a special pleasure or *vertù* was to be had through the ability of mind (*acutezza*) to experience and understand an artifact as a labyrinth, an intricate space of signification. There exists an implicit affinity between such a view and the pre-Cartesian concepts of mind and language use which begin to appear in late sixteenth-century psychology. In Spain, Juan de Huarte's popular *Examen de ingenios* (1575), a book there is every reason to suppose that Góngora knew as intimately as did Cervantes (who used it for *El licenciado Vidriera*), had emphasized the capacity of intelligence, operating through language, to "speak such subtle and surprising things, yet true, that were never before seen, heard, or writ, no, nor ever so much as thought of."[11] Tasso's legitimization in his *Discorsi* of *meraviglia*, "impossible" metaphors, followed a similar logic in suggesting that poetic language not only represents something in the world but also creates realities proper to the imagination. On the other hand, the leitmotif of Cascales and the *detractores* was, precisely, that the *Soledades* betrayed a contradiction of form and content, of language and that which language represents—the Scholastic entailment of *res* and *verba*. Hence they saw the catachresis, the figure of rhetoric in which language is strained beyond its ability to communicate, to make sense, as the paradigm of Góngora's poetry. By seeming to posit conceptual wit (*ingenio*) as the primary basis for aesthetic appreciation, they felt, Góngora was immoral, producing a poetics which embodied neither the pleasing nor the useful.[12]

Góngora in return, however, seems in the "Carta en respuesta" intent on making this problem of representation, of the way in which language signifies, the major theme of this defense (and his major instruction to the reader). He admits that the *Soledades* are unreadable in an ordinary sense. They can only be approached through a process of speculation, a process that holds its own pleasure:

> Deleitable tiene lo que en los dos puntos de arriba queda explicado, pues si deleitar el entendimiento es darle razones que la concluyan y se midan con su contento, descubierto lo que está debajo de esos tropos, por fuerza el entendimiento ha de quedar convencido, y convencido, satisfecho; demás que, como el fin del entendimiento es hacer presa en verdades, que por eso no le satisface nada, si no es la primera verdad, conforme a aquella sentencia de San Agustín: *Inquietum est cor nostrum, donec requiescat in te*, en tanto quedará más deleitado cuanto, obligándole a la especulación por la obscuridad de la obra, fuera hallando debajo de las sombras de la obscuridad asimilaciones a su concepto. (Millé, Epistolario 2)

Discussing the final clause of this passage, Jones took the "su" of "asimilaciones a su concepto" to refer to "la primera verdad." Thus, he read the clause as "asimilaciones al concepto de la primera verdad," which, in association with the tag from Augustine, yields God and, for Jones, the idea of the poem as a Platonic mimesis of "the principles on which the world is founded." But this "su" is syntactically ambiguous. The "fin del entendimiento" Góngora is claiming for the reader laboring over his "tropos" may be reflexive; that is, the "asimilaciones a su concepto" which intelligence is to find in the exercise the figures require may also be, in one sense, "asimilaciones al concepto que el entendimiento tiene de sí mismo." The conceit involves an amphibology, characteristic of Góngora's style in other contexts, which equates with "su concepto" both "la primera verdad" and "entendimiento."[13]

"Deleitar el entendimiento"–the concept prefigures the Neo-Scholastic aesthetics later worked out by Gracián in the *Agudeza y arte de ingenio* (1642). Gracián grants that intelligence pleases itself both in the construction and deciphering of conceits; but in this ability and activity it tacitly mirrors the nature of a divinity which makes itself, like the conceit, "manifiesto y escondido" in its creation. For Gracián, the artifice of poetic invention and conceptual wit always has the value of revealing in its estrangement of ordinary discourse the esoteric text of a *scripturas Dei*. The conceit, no matter how fanciful or artificial, *reads out* the theological book of creation in a relationship of microcosm (mind and language use) to a macrocosm (God, sufficient reason) which sustains its being and its truth. The intelligence of the poet has an active role to play in creation by showing the hidden resemblances God has "written into" the nature of things.

There remains, however, an important difference between the calculated ambiguity of Góngora's letter and Gracián's theological formalism. Unlike Cascales and the defenders of post-Tridentine poetics, Gracián can accept the idea of poetry as a spectacle of wit because wit is a natural property of mind and mind is always the semblance of its creator and the means of apprehending the subtle logic of his creation. The point of an "arte de ingenio" is to learn how to know (and therefore be like) the idea of God. Góngora touches on this position in his "su concepto" amphibology, but the *Soledades* are not an exercise in religious enlightenment. Rather the problems they pose and the attitude of mind that is required to solve them seems a rigorously secular one, and Gracián's appreciation of Góngora a belated attempt to win for Christian dogmatics a poetry that seems quite content, at least in the *Soledades*, to leave matters of religion "in parenthesis."[14]

The influence of Mannerist theory and example was already evident in Spain in the poetry of Herrera and his school and the new tendencies in painting and music represented by figures like El Greco or Luis de Victoria towards the end of the sixteenth century. Góngora must have read with special care, however, the slim *Libro de la erudición poética* (1611) by his fellow Andalusian Luis Carrillo y Sotomayor. The treatise is a meditation on the relation of poetry and philosophy, which Plato, notably in the *Republic*, had posed as a contradiction. Carrillo y Sotomayor wanted to construct a defense of poetry as a specific form of knowledge, an "erudición." He recalls in the *Libro* the Greek *poiein*–to make or construct–hence *poeisis* as creative power, creative act. "Filósofos fueron los Poetas antiguos, y despreciando animosamente después las cosas naturales, emprendieron a las que la misma naturaleza no se atreve."[15] (This recalls Juan de Huarte's etymological argument that wit–*ingenio*–and *engendrar* have the same root in the Latin *genere*: hence wit as a "generative power.") Lucretius' *De rerum natura* serves as an example. In his account of the creation as material accident, Lucretius, claims Carrillo y Sotomayor, ignores the Christian (and so dogmatic) understanding of the origin and order of nature: "Notable atrevimiento le dió el arte, pues con ella quiso confundir la cosa más evidente de la naturaleza, negava la providencia. . . ."[16] But this error, which is after all the very principle of Lucretian mimesis, does not invalidate the poem, which remains a model of "doctas dificultades." The point is that poetry in itself constitutes for Carrillo y Sotomayor a legitimate mode of understanding the world (an "acto del entendimiento," to use Góngora's phrase) which may produce a true knowledge of things in ways independent, because of the free nature of poetic inspiration and creation, of matters of dogma, common sense, or verisimiltude in its strict sense. By definition, poetry is necessarily "para los pocos," those few spirits with the special intelligence and sensitivity to read it on its own terms. Góngora seems to derive directly from this aristocratic humanism when he claims in the "Carta en respuesta":

> . . . honra me ha causado hacerme escuro a los ignorantes, que esa [es] la distinción de los hombres doctos, hablar de manera que a ellos les parezca griego; pues no se han de dar las piedras preciosas a animales de cerda: y bien dije griego, locución exquisita que viene de *Poeses*, verbo de aquella lengua madre de las ciencias. . . .[17]

I want to turn for a moment from this exposition of the literary problematic addressed in the "Carta" to study two passages from the *Soledad primera* by way of showing the relation between the kind of positions Góngora takes there and his actual practice in the poem. The first represents the cellular level of the *Soledades*: Góngora's construction of a single syntactic and imagistic period, a "tropo." The example I have chosen is a burlesque periphrasis in the dinner the pilgrim shares with the goatherds of the "bienaventurado albergue":

> *El que de cabras fué dos veces ciento*
> *esposo casi un lustro*–cuyo diente
> no perdonó a racimo aun en la frente
> de Baco, cuanto más en su sarmiento–
> (triunfador siempre de celosas lides,
> lo coronó el Amor; mas rival tierno
> breve de barba y duro no de cuerno,
> redimió con su muerte tantas vides)
> *servido ya en cecina*
> *purpúreos hilos es de grana fina.* (I, 153-62)

The passage typifies Góngora's recourse to effects of mordant irony as a relief from the elevated epico-lyrical mode of the poem. It is built on two coextensive hyperbatons. One is the dilation of the normal predication form of the sentence, rendered in italics above, by the double parenthesis ("cuyo diente" to "sarmiento" / "triunfador" to "vides"), a dilation which is further complicated by the allusion to Bacchus. Second is the formation of the sentence as an enigma: the identity of the initial subject "el que"–the goat–is not disclosed until the end when it has been transformed into an object, the slices of meat eaten by the pilgrim and his hosts. As Spitzer pointed out in a classic note on this passage, the semantic metamorphosis takes us from the sexually potent live goat (the "esposo") devouring plants to the dead goat himself devoured as "purpúreos hilos."[18] Once the absent center of the figure becomes evident, that is, the idea of a "macho cabrío," the dilated period abruptly composes itself. The spiral of the double parenthesis, which involves an intricate amplification of the theme by drawing in the myth of Bacchus and the scene of the old and young goats fighting over a mate in "celosas lides," terminates neatly in "servido ya en cecina." But the old goat receives in his sudden fall from erotic plenitude a kind of ennobling epitaph: "purpúreos hilos es de grana fina." Spitzer took this cyclical invention on the prosaic datum of the goat meat as typifying, in its disjunction of linguistic apparatus and topical content, Góngora's sense of the "corteza"-"misterioso" relation. "Se trata aquí de un juego puramente intelectual de relaciones percibidas entre la carne y el animal," he noted. "El barroquismo de Góngora se complace en *dorar con una belleza facticia un espectáculo que por sí mismo desilusiona* [italics mine]. . . ."[19]

But this "system" is precisely artificial because it is discrete. In contrast, I want to move now to one of the most extended metaphoric periphrases in the poem, the variations on the "breve esplendor de mal distinta lumbre" which occupy lines 52 to 94 of the *Soledad primera*. Briefly, the context of this passage is that the pilgrim, having rescued himself from the shipwreck, ascends a cliff along the coast and at the summit spies a distant glimmer of light towards which he directs his footsteps in the gathering darkness. R. O. Jones saw this as an allegory "representing, in fact, a passage from error to truth."[20] The first vision of the light appears after the confusion of the first scenes of the poem (the storm, shipwreck, and twilight):

> Vencida al fin la cumbre
> –del mar siempre sonante,
> de la muda campaña
> árbitro igual e inexpugnable muro–,
> con pie ya más seguro
> declina al vacilante
> breve esplendor de *mal distinta lumbre*. (52-58)

The subsequent movement towards the light will be inland, forming an anabasis which will continue until the pilgrim reappears on the shore at the beginning of the *Soledad segunda*. Jones: "the imagery changes–naturally, one might say, since he leaves the sea behind."[21]

The light seems first to the pilgrim a "farol de una cabaña." The bucolic image is, however, immediately metamorphosed into a piscatory or nautical context, as if it were a light anchored ("que sobre el ferro está") in a gulf of shadows, like the beacon of a lightship signaling a port. This movement of the image refers us back to the initial scene of the shipwreck. Góngora extends it in the following verses in which the pilgrim addresses the light, speaking in his own voice for the first time in the poem:

> "Rayos–les dice–ya que no de Leda
> trémulos hijos, sed de mi fortuna
> término luminoso." . . . (62-64)

The construction is what we have learned to recognize from Dámaso Alonso's studies as Góngora's characteristic "si no A, B." The "ya que no de Leda" alludes to the fire of Saint Elmo which makes the masts and rigging of a ship glow with static energy (there is a famous scene in *Moby Dick* describing this), here associated with Leda's sons, Castor and Pollux, and the star constellation of Gemini named after them. In nautical lore, the sons of Leda signify a providential presence in the midst of a storm. But as the pilgrim is now on land, he intends the nautical allusion as a metaphor for what he hopes the light will reveal, a "de mi fortuna / término luminoso." (Spitzer speculated that a double sense of "fortuna" is intended here: the ordinary fate or fortune and the secondary meaning of "fortuna" in Spanish as storm.) As the pilgrim moves towards the source of the light, this ambiguity between nautical and terrestrial contexts will be kept alive by phrases like "golfo de sombras," "norte de su aguja," "la arboleda cruja" (like rigging in a storm). As Spitzer pointed out, "El fuego de San Telmo tiembla como todo en un barco, el 'término' participa de la solidez y fijeza del continente."[22]

The next section, 64-83, begins to transpose the image of the light into its proper context, that of the land. (The shift is marked by the caesura forced by the period in line 64.)

> . . . Y–recelando
> de invidïosa bárbara arboleda
> interposición, cuando
> de vientos no conjuración alguna–
> *cual*, haciendo el villano
> la fragosa montaña fácil llano,
> atento sigue aquella
> –aun a pesar de las tinieblas bella,
> aun a pesar de las estrellas clara–
> piedra, indigna tiara
> –si tradición apócrifa no miente–
> de animal tenebroso, cuya frente
> carro es brillante de nocturno día:
> *tal*, diligente, el paso
> el joven apresura,
> midiendo la espesura
> con igual pie que el raso,
> fijo–a despecho de la niebla fría–
> en el carbunclo, norte de su aguja,
> o el Austro brame o la arboleda cruja.

The "tal-cual" construction marks an inner periphrasis in this involuted period. Where before, the light had seemed a port beacon in a storm, now it has become a "carbunclo" or ruby, that is, an artifact drawn from the depths of the earth, which the pilgrim follows like a hunter or peasant "midiendo la espesura." The "animal tenebroso" could be the tiger shining in the night (as in Blake's ballad), the mystic stag whose antlers form a candelabra in the moonlight, or "carro brillante de nocturno día" in a nocturnal inversion of the myth of Phaeton. The analogy of the pilgrim and the hunter suggests also his character as a Petrarchan hero, the lover "shipwrecked" in his affections and abandoned in a night of solitary despair, now striving towards the beams of light emitted by the distant beloved.[23]

A dog suddenly appears to accompany the wanderer. The "mal distinta lumbre" of the beginning now reveals itself to be an oak trunk burning in the center of a rustic shelter where he will find the domestic repose ("cabaña") prefigured in his mind when he first glimpsed the light. As in the smaller case of the inventions on the goat meat, the closure of the whole sequence is again, after the elaborate syntactic and allusive metamorphosis which must have sent more than one reader back to his library, abrupt and epitaphic:

> El can ya, vigilante,
> convoca, despidiendo al caminante;
> y la que *desviada*
> luz poca pareció, tanta es *vecina*,
> que yace en ella la robusta encina
> mariposa en cenizas desatada. (84-89)

Why this taste for periphrasis? I want to suggest that it is not only an aesthetic decor—a "puro placer de formas"—but also a way of establishing the narrative context of the pilgrim and the psychagogic task of the reader which Góngora outlines in the proposition of the *Soledades*:

> Pasos de un peregrino son errante
> cuantos me dictó versos dulce musa:
> en soledad confusa
> perdidos unos, otros inspirados.

Maurice Molho, in a detailed analysis of this proposition, sees it as constructed on two parallel planes of reference—that of the poet-creator, that of the pilgrim-actor—both of which, in turn, invoke the *tertium quid* of the reader. The amphibology between these two planes creates four relations of equivalence between a total of eight semantic elements: (1) the *pasos* of the pilgrim and the *versos* of the poet (e.g., meter as "pies" in many figures of the poem); (2) the poet and his *persona*, both "peregrino errante"; (3) the "soledad confusa" of the poem-poet (its obscurity and the *silva* form itself) and of the hero, lovesick and abandoned in a wilderness or "selva"; (4) the *pasos* and the *versos*, alternately *perdidos* ("en soledad confusa") or *inspirados* (by the "dulce musa"). The last relation suggests a kind of auto-criticism: some of the passages of the poem are "logrados," finished, others (the whole poem itself) are not.[24]

The "versos" or script (the "corteza" of the letter) move in the sequence of variations on the light exactly as the pilgrim towards its source. The syntactic complication of 64-83, created by the proliferation of relative clauses, mimics the difficulty the pilgrim has in walking on a wild and uncertain terrain and losing sight of the light through an "invidiosa bárbara arboleda interposición" and the evening fog. The development, in other words, takes place along two axially related poles. The periphrasis defines the implicit *psychology* of the pilgrim, compounding around the visual datum a whole trajectory of memory, anxiety, and hope ("recelando"). It also follows a spatial logic in which the progressive metamorphoses of the light correspond to its changing visual character as the pilgrim approaches it. (In line 82, for example, it has become a ruby that has acquired something of the redness of the dying fire disclosed at the end.) The "luz poca" becomes in this double process emblematic of luminosity–the Platonic image of the numinous–in the expanding network of metaphors and allusions made possible by the relativity of the pilgrim's spatial and sentimental perspectives. This expansion finds its necessary closure in the recognition of the actual source of the light which involves yet another metamorphosis, that of the tree into flame and ashes. This recognition, in turn, is isochronic with the pilgrim's arrival at the *albergue* and the end (in "mariposa en cenizas desatada") of the sequence which had begun in the confusion of land and sea and the "trémulos hijos."

As he will throughout the poem, Góngora has taken care to mark within this process the line of movement in space and time of his hero: "con pie ya más seguro / declina . . . ," "cual, haciendo el villano / la fragosa montaña fácil llano," "midiendo la espesura / con igual pie que el raso," "y la que desviada / luz poca pareció, tanta es vecina," "Llegó pues, el mancebo. . . ." This movement is homologous with that of the reader who has been treading through the "selva" of the poem's language. These images are, on the one hand, part of what the reader must understand and, on the other, a representation of what he is going through in coming to this understanding: "vacilando el entendimiento en fuerza del discurso, trabajándole (pues crece con cualquier acto de valor), alcance lo que así en la lectura superficial de sus versos no pudo entender" (Millé, Epistolario 2).

In the two passages we have considered, the obscurity Góngora produces is dependent not only on the difficulty of interpreting the images and allusions, but also on the complications of the syntax in which they are framed. There is a section in the "Carta" where Góngora takes up the question of the possible extent of syntagmatic freedom in discourse. The critic(s) of the "Carta de un amigo" had spoken of him as "inventor de dificultar la construcción de el romance," suggesting that this effort had been a "disparate." Góngora replied to the effect that he had not transgressed but rather enriched the system of rules affecting the mental coherence of language:

> [Es] lance forzoso venerar que nuestra lengua a costa de mi trabajo haya llegado a la perfección y alteza de la latina, a quien no he quitado los artículos, como le parece a V.m. y esos señores, sino excusándolos donde no necesarios: y ansí gustaré me dijese en dónde faltan o qué razón de ella no está corriente en lenguaje heroico (que ha de ser diferente de la prosa y digno de personas capaces de entendelle); que holgaré construírselo, aunque niego no poder ligar el romance a esas declinaciones. . . . (Millé, Epistolario 2)

In Scholastic rhetoric the term for hyperbaton as a figure of syntax is *transgressio*. The problem Góngora is addressing here is a technical one: how can one expand the signifying capacity of language within its rules? What is the limit beyond which language ceases to signify, becomes Babelic?[25] But this problem is also a feature of the thematic content of the *Soledades* which is everywhere a posing of images of overabundance, chaos and violence against the reiterated convention of a golden mean of synthesis and harmony, the bucolic *mediocritas*. Góngora presents not only language alone but language which has been invested with the capacity to contain an ethical, political, and ecological meditation on the proper relation of nature and society, of authority and freedom, of love–a meditation conducted through the prism of the historical crisis he lives through in his own fortune as a poet and courtier.

> Piloto hoy la Codicia, no de errantes
> árboles, mas de selvas inconstantes,
> al padre de las aguas Oceäno
> –de cuya monarquía
> el Sol, que cada día
> nace en sus ondas y en sus ondas muere,
> *los términos saber todos no quiere*–
> dejó primero de su espuma cano,
> sin admitir segundo
> *en inculcar sus límites al mundo.* (I, 403-12)

A passage like this (which is taken from the epic fragment on the explorations and conquests of the sixteenth century which Góngora interpolates in the Arcadian scenery of the first *Soledad*) strategically intertwines the event that is being represented and the mode of language that is doing the representing. "Saber términos," "inculcar límites": these are the problems Góngora must struggle with in his construction of the *Soledades*, his own "selva inconstante." The danger, as in the crisis of empire itself, is that ambitious desire will produce transgression and perversion. But the other side of the wager is the possibility of a language of *discovery*. The economics of art replace here the economics of an imperial project that has become problematic, no longer yields the expected wealth and power.[26]

Góngora mentions three languages or modes of language in the letter: (1) Latin and Greek, (2) a "lenguaje heroico"–poetic (or prophetic) language, and (3) "el romance"–prose or ordinary language. Spanish, like the other European national languages of the Renaissance, would be, in the judgement of Góngora's aristocratic humanism, a language fallen from grace, from the "perfección y alteza de la latina." Góngora's labor (and by extension the reader's) is to have sublimated ordinary Spanish by incorporating into it the complicated periods of Latin syntax. "El romance" thus attains the status of a sublime discourse in the *Soledades* because it has now become, Góngora is implying, an instrument for knowing and feeling the many contingencies and alternatives of Spain's social and national destiny: an "imperial" language which expresses an anti-imperialist ethics. The poet's work, fashioned in exile from the Court and the centers of wealth and power, "causarme ha autoridad" because it is, like the Latin political essay or ode, a formal paradigm of the measured subtlety and innovation required by civic policy. (Milton will make the same claim for his *Paradises*.)

The equation which is implicit throughout Góngora's self-defense is of the mastery of language and of the mastery of government. The poet-*vates* is the poet as *legislator*. The danger of excess, of a "fall" into nonsense, is its necessary risk, the poet's gamble on the page, just as the adventure in the space and time of the world pictured in the interpolated epic involves the risk of death or disaster. But Góngora is posing his poem *against* the disaster of Spain's imperialism. His language is expanded ("los términos saber no quiere") to represent the nature of a complex historical time and space; but it is also salvaged before it disintegrates into chaos. Góngora begins by placing before the reader/pilgrim a datum, then amplifies it in a geometric play of figures of identity and difference, so passing continually from the *cornucopia*–the world as a spiral of illusion, confused variety–to the linear sequence of the "pasos" to, finally, the moment when the sense of the whole reveals itself, the moment of enlightenment, of the "misterioso," but also of the closure or representation: to the figure as a *tomb*.

> "Túmulo tanto debe
> agradecido Amor a mi pie errante;
> líquido, pues, diamante
> calle mis huesos, y elevada cima
> selle sí, mas no oprima,
> esta que le fiaré ceniza breve,
> si hay ondas mudas y si hay tierra leve." (II, 165-71)

The *Soledades* are not allegory in the sense of being a presentation of details which mechanically convert, point by point, into a second order of signification; to assume this was the mistake made, for example, by Serrano de Paz in his *Comentarios*. On the other hand they are not a "puro placer de formas" either. Rather they are a process where the questions of "making poetry" have become involved with the historical reality this making reflects, both as a means of representation and as a process in which a poetics transforms itself into an ethics. This landscape of world exhaustion, of the death of the signifier, predicts again and again in the individual "tropos" the ultimate self-exhaustion of the poem itself in the terminal epitaph "y a la estigia deidad con bella esposa." This dialectic of freedom and necessity, of historical tragedy and the precarious grace of poetry to oppose it, forms the inner sense of one of the most extraordinary passages in all of Góngora's poetry, the description of a river viewed by the pilgrim from a mountain lookout, as it appears in the earliest manuscript copies of the *Soledad primera*:

> Si mucho poco mapa le despliega,
> mucho es más lo que, nieblas desatando,
> confunde el sol y la distancia niega.
> Muda la admiración, habla callando,
> y, ciega, un río sigue, que–luciente
> de aquellos montes hijo–
> con torcido discurso, si prolijo,
> tiraniza los campos útilmente;
> orladas sus orillas de frutales,
> si de flores, tomadas, no, a la Aurora
> derecho corre mientras no revoca
> los mismos autos el de sus cristales;
> huye un trecho de sí, y se alcanza luego;
> desvíase, y, buscando sus desvíos,
> errores dulces, dulces desvaríos,
> hacen sus aguas con lascivo juego;
> engazando edificios en su plata,
> de quintas coronado, se dilata
> majestuosamente
> –en brazos dividido caudalosos
> de islas, que paréntesis frondosos
> al período son de su corriente–
> de la alta gruta donde se desata
> hasta los jaspes líquidos, adonde
> su orgullo pierde y su memoria esconde. (Cf. Millé, I, 194-211)

Góngora's mentor and friend, Pedro de Valencia, had him censor this passage when he prepared the canonic text of the *Soledades*.[27] But the ingenious equation of the course of the river with the figuration of a rhetorical period and the consequent isomorphism of the sentence and that which it describes may stand by itself as a miniature of the poem, of a language of time: Gracián's "el curso de tu vida en un discurso," Joyce's "riverrun past Eve and Adam." The scene is something apprehended as a totality, a map, just as the linguistic territory of the *Soledades* is meant to be mapped by the critical work of the reader. Walter Benjamin saw the Baroque conception of history as a *Trauerspiel*, a representation, at once a tragedy or funeral procession and a triumph, in which the world passes in review and is petrified into signs under the organizing gaze of melancholy.[28] In the *Soledades*, Góngora deploys a language which seeks to be reconciled and find consummation with an object of desire–the pilgrim's alienated mistress, the receptive intelligence of the reader, the mind of his country. The spatial frontier of exile, the wilderness which is the landscape dimension of the pilgrim's search, is also the boundary between the poem as a *utopia* of language and Cascales' *Babel*, the disintegration of language and mind, the descent of discourse into madness.

2

"Soledad primera," Lines 1–61: The Pilgrim

We can see, then, that metaphor occurs at the precise point at which sense comes out of non-sense, that is, at the frontier which, as Freud discovered, when crossed the other way produces what we generally call 'wit' (Witz)*; it is at this frontier that man tempts his very destiny when he derides the signifier.*

Jacques Lacan
"The Insistence of the Letter"

When moisture
Unites with heat, life is conceived; all things
Come from this union. Fire may fight with water,
But heat and moisture generate all things,
Their discord being productive.

Ovid
Metamorphoses (trans. Humphries)

No los confundió Dios a ellos con darles lenguaje confuso, sino en el mismo suyo ellos se confundieron, tomando piedra por agua, y agua por piedra. . . .

Góngora
"Carta en respuesta"

There is throughout Góngora's poetry a constant attraction to the sea; more concretely, it tends to explore over and over the boundary between earth and water–"la incierta ribera"–the play of tide and surf, the vision of land becoming water, water giving way to land:

Muros desmantelando, pues, de arena,
centauro ya espumoso el Ocëano
–medio mar, medio ría–
dos veces huella la campaña al día (II, 9-12)

This setting permits the activation of the themes of the sea and navigation. Góngora, like Herrera and Carrillo y Sotomayor before him (and unlike Garcilaso from whose pastoral the sea is absent), is the poet of an imperial Spain whose open frontier and whose destiny is an "Océano importuno":

> . . . ese teatro de Fortuna
> descubro, ese voraz, ese profundo
> campo ya de sepulcros, que, sediento,
> cuanto, en vasos de abeto, Nuevo Mundo
> –tributos digo américos–se bebe
> en túmulos de espuma paga breve. (II, 401-06)

Along the shoreline, the human and historical pathos of a ruined empire is set against the ceaseless generation and regeneration of nature. It is a genesis landscape subject to the play of universal energy, the ebb and flow of tide, the vagaries of wind and wave, sun and storm, in which the four elements appear as "confused": Gracián's "mundo trabucado," "the world turned upside down": the Baroque *adynata*.

The shoreline frames the intricate tragedy of Acis and Galatea in the *Polifemo*. Like the pilgrim, Acis appears on a shore where the Sicilian sea "el pie argenta de plata al Lilibeo." Crushed by the rock of Polyphemus, his body flows back to the beach and the sea, "corriente plata al fin sus blancos huesos." It is also the reference landscape of the *Soledades*, introducing both of the two cantos and defining the space of the hawking scenes and the indefinite ending of the poem. Saturated with mythic allusions, it composes an epico-lyrical stage on which the lovesick pilgrim acts out his double role as protagonist of the representation and subject of the teleonomic movement of language.

The dynamics of this shoreline landscape establish the presence of the pilgrim in the *Soledades*. With the appearance of the "mal distinta lumbre" in line 58, the pilgrim leaves the shoreline to move inland towards the pastoral apotheosis of the wedding scenes. The section dealt with here is the opening depiction of his shipwreck and salvation from the sea: lines 1-61 of the *Soledad primera*. Dámaso Alonso divided this sequence in his 1927 edition of the *Soledades* into seven periods: (1) 1-14 (the shipwreck), (2) 15-21 (rescue on a wooden plank), (3) 22-28 (surf and shoreline), (4) 29-33 (the pilgrim reaches land), (5) 34-41 (ritual drying of his clothes), (6) 42-51 (ascension of the shoreline cliffs), and (7) 52-61 (view of the scene from above). This arrangement has been followed since it is the one found in most modern editions of the *Soledades*.[1]

The *Soledades* begin *in medias res* with an image of a turbulent chaos of nature and the universe:

> Era del año la estación florida
> en que el mentido robador de Europa
> –media luna las armas de su frente,
> y el Sol todos los rayos de su pelo–,
> luciente honor del cielo,

en campos de zafiro pace estrellas;
cuando el que ministrar podía la copa
a Júpiter mejor que el garzón de Ida,
–náufrago y desdeñado, sobre ausente–
lagrimosas de amor dulces querellas
da al mar; que condolido,
fué a las ondas, fué al viento
el mísero gemido,
segundo de Arión dulce instrumento.

This opening period, 1-14, is broken into two partially independent sentences by the semicolon at the end of 6. The first pictures the cosmic light of the universe against the blue of a late afternoon sky; the second, the struggle of the pilgrim on the surface of the stormy sea. The seasonal mode is spring, "la estación florida" –the time of nature's rebirth, the Age of Saturn. Góngora's celebrated allusion to the constellation of Taurus equates violence of rebirth with the image of the sun as source of cosmic energy and the bull as symbol of sexuality. In spring the sun enters the planetary house of Taurus; this yields "y el Sol todos los rayos de su pelo." The moon is simultaneously present as "media luna las armas de su frente," an ellipsis describing the sky of late afternoon when sun, moon, and the early evening stars are already visible in the deep blue ("campos de zafiro") of the upper atmosphere. Combined with the sun, Taurus represents the primary element of fire; this is connected in the allusion to the image of the bull as the anthropomorphic form which the god Jupiter assumes to abduct and rape Europa –hence "*mentido* robador." The story of the rape of Europa involves sequentially, in Ovid's systematization of Classical myth, the beginning of the pilgrimage of Cadmus, her brother, who sets out to find her. His departure initiates the Theban cycle, which will many years later terminate in the foundation of the city. The rape, on the other hand, signifies the primeval dance of matter, the genesis of nature. The sexual antagonism of Jupiter and Europa, expressed in the cosmic violence of spring and storm, will be resolved on the level of the human protagonists by the "yugo" of the wedding ceremony which ends the first *Soledad*. The implicit presence of Cadmus in the opening drama carries the emotion of a fraternal, human love opposed to the erotic deceit of the bull.[2]

The semicolon after the transposed pastoral scene of the bull grazing in the stars halts the spiraling catachresis. The division marks the sudden shift of visual perspective from the receding infinity of the universe to the human drama of the pilgrim struggling in the waves. Europa is seduced on the shoreline and carried up to the heavens in a tragic apotheosis; the pilgrim falls into history like Cadmus with "lagrimosas de amor dulces querellas." The shipwreck is the *desastre* of Byzantine romance, the *separation* of the fraternal love of man and woman, brother and sister: the loss of the sheltering homeland. The pilgrim enters a world that he must begin to master and recreate. The allusion to Ganymede suggests the homosexual ideal of adolescent male beauty: Europa is the female and human object of Jupiter's desire, at once divine and animal;

Ganymede, the *puer*. To abduct Europa, the god takes the form of the bull (animal of the earth); to seduce Ganymede, he assumes the form of the eagle (animal of the air). Like his doubles Cadmus and Ganymede, the pilgrim bears within himself a new sense of *difference* and *absence*, a psychic division into opposing or perverted terms: "–náufrago y desdeñado, sobre ausente–." Jupiter is the figure of the mature man, the father-procreator, the pilgrim, the adolescent who has been violated, who has discovered his loss of innocence: "el mancebo," "garzón," "inconsiderado peregrino." His tears and cries are the expression of the violence he feels within himself. Extending outwards as a "dulce instrumento" they conjoin with their natural harmonies, water and air: "fué a las ondas, fué al viento." Behind the sentimental and natural chaos is Venus, the "absent" woman, the mother, the goddess of the sea-farer who is "condolido" with the pilgrim. Arion is the orphic poet, like the pilgrim abandoned and drowning in the ocean, shipwrecked. The pilgrim's lament is "segundo de Arión dulce instrumento" in the sense that it will, like Arion's lyre, like the poem itself, seduce through art the goddess of providence and erotic harmony. If the first part of the period concerned the element of fire in the image of Jupiter, the second implicitly contains Venus, the spirit of water.

Taken together, the two periods that follow, 15-21 and 22-28, are syntactically isomorphic with the first. But where 1-14 needs the semicolon to contain and carry over the tissue of allusion which composes the storm and shipwreck, the latter form two independent sentences and narrative moments of six and seven lines respectively. The first represents the effects of the pilgrim's "querellas" which have moved Venus to mediate the violence of the storm and provide an instrument of rescue:

> Del siempre en la montaña opuesto pino
> al enemigo Noto,
> piadoso miembro roto
> –breve tabla–delfín no fué pequeño
> al inconsiderado peregrino
> que a una Libia de ondas su camino
> fió, y su vida a un leño.

The syntactic break in the first period organized the opposition of the elements of fire and water; the second begins with a graphic image of the struggle of earth and air, the mountain pine standing against the storm wind ("enemigo Noto"). The period develops around a typically Gongorist amphibology. We can read here that either a piece of wood ("piadoso miembro") torn from the pine by the storm or a "tabla" (the pine fashioned into a plank) torn loose from the wreckage of the ship, becomes a dolphin or instrument of salvation for the drowning pilgrim. The "delfín no fue pequeño," apparently totally peripheral, is a logical extension of the identification of the pilgrim with Arion. (Wishing to visit his birthplace–he is a son of Polyphemus–Arion embarks.

The crew of his ship decide to kill him for his riches. He entreats them to listen to his music and then plunges into the sea. A number of dolphins attracted by his music appear to rescue him, one of them carrying him to shore.) The conceit depends on the intertwining of a number of different elements: pine and mountain (earth) against wind (air); pine as wood in nature against pine as "leño," the conventional synecdoche for ship (Pellicer: "Allí *pino* está tomado por la nave"); wood as inanimate against the dolphin as animate (and semi-human).[3] The terminal "una Libia de ondas su camino" complements the initial earth-air antithesis with an image of reversed natural order built on the conceited identity, or *correspondencia*, of the desert as an extreme of dehydration and the waves as an excess of water, both dimensions of disaster for an "inconsiderado peregrino."

> Del Océano pues antes sorbido,
> y luego vomitado
> no lejos de un escollo coronado
> de secos juncos, de calientes plumas,
> –alga todo y espumas–
> halló hospitalidad donde halló nido
> de Júpiter el ave. (I, 22-28)

The pivotal moment is the "halló hospitalidad" which cancels the "–náufrago y desdeñado, sobre ausente–" of the first period. The pilgrim reaches the surfline; he is first ingested ("sorbido") by the undertow, then expelled ("vomitado") by the surf onto the shore "no lejos de un escollo." This shore cliff, which will (55) become "árbitro igual e inexpugnable muro," marks the exact demarcation between earth and water. (The beach is "uncertain.") Where the hero's disaster is descensional (the "fall" of the shipwreck), his pilgrimage must begin with an ascension of the cliff. This is suggested by the image (from below) of the crown of dry rushes and warm feathers, the nest of the eagle ("ave de Júpiter"). The "secos juncos" and "calientes plumas" of the summit resonate with the "Libia" of the second unit as forms of heat and dehydration, but now evoke emotions of hospitality and shelter. On the beach below, the pilgrim emerges covered with "alga" (seaweed, green plant life like the rushes) and "espumas" (seafoam, white like the warm feathers). The spatial antithesis of summit and base is thus converted into a partial identity by the equation of the nest with the shoreline which shelters the pilgrim from the "Libia de ondas." (The eagle is the animal metamorphosis which Jupiter assumed to seduce Ganymede.) The bull and the eagle (as forms of Jupiter) combine with the dolphin (as animal of Venus) to encode the interplay of the four elements: the bull as an animal of earth metamorphosed into the sun, the wood on land becoming a dolphin in water, the nest of the eagle emblematizing the pilgrim's return to his proper element, the earth.

Góngora rarely names Venus directly in the *Soledades*. Nevertheless we sense that her presence hovers over the solitude of the self-destructive pilgrim. The signifier for her presence is the curious rhyme of "pluma" and "espuma" which is repeated throughout the poem, here to link the feathers of the nest above with the foam of the sea below. The key is revealed in the final couplet of the *Soledad primera* which celebrates the sexual union of two young peasants:

> bien previno la hija de la espuma
> a batallas de amor campo de pluma.

"Espuma" derives from *aphrogeneia*, "born of the foam," an epithet for the name Venus in Greek, Aphrodite. (Hence her role as goddess of fortune for sailors and her relation with the dolphin.) The "calientes plumas" drift from their initial reference to Jupiter's eagle to become, inversely, a synecdoche for the bird of Venus, the peaceful dove—that is, for the mediation of discord in nature or in the psyche.

In part, the symbolism of Venus/Aphrodite as a humanizing and feminizing force behind the blind violence of nature depends on her position in the intricate kinship system of Classical mythology. She is Jupiter's daughter, consequently in a fraternal relation with Apollo, Mars, Diana, Bacchus, Mercury, Minerva, and so forth. As the wife of Vulcan, she is sexually joined to a half-brother. For Virgil, she is the divine mother who silently protects and supervises the *Aeneid*; like Cadmus and the pilgrim, Aeneas is the "fallen" adolescent who must rediscover or recreate his home.[4]

Venus is then the sister/mother, the sea as *mater genetrix*; Jupiter the father, the bull or eagle as masculine sexual violence and destructive force; Cadmus/Ganymede/Europa the violated consciousness of the dependent adolescent. In his soliloquy in the *Soledad segunda*, the pilgrim represents his own fate as that of an Icarus:

> "Audaz mi pensamiento
> el cenit escaló, *plumas* vestido,
> cuyo vuelo atrevido
> —si no ha dado su nombre a tus *espumas*—
> de sus vestidas *plumas*
> conservarán el desvanecimiento
> los anales diáfanos del viento." (II, 137-43)

Icarus signifies the violation through an excess of desire of the ethical norm of *mediocritas*, prudence and moderation: the dream of sun (flight); the dream of water (enclosure).[5] The ambition to fly into the sun represents the overcoming of the father, Daedalus, who has fashioned the very means of this overcoming; the Oedipal catastrophe inherent in the impulse leads inversely, like the pilgrim's shipwreck, into the sea as mother: softness, wetness, embrace. ("¡Oh mar, oh tú, supremo / moderador piadoso de mis daños!"–II, 123-24) We are meant to understand by the "desdeñado" of I, 9 that the pilgrim is the Petrarchan paradigm of a lovesick consciousness. His sea voyage is a flight into free space (and danger: "inconsiderado"), away from but also towards the alienated woman, the "enemiga amada" who is the source both of his loss of harmony and its restoration in the future towards which his pilgrimage points. He bears, that is, a psychic disintegration–an absence–manifested through a crisis of language itself, a confusion of the signifier, the fall of discourse into catachresis or *non-sense*. The divided ego exteriorizes its trauma in the binary labyrinth of the genetic landscape.

Michel Foucault has noted the affinity which obtains between the sea and madness in the medieval institution of the *Stultifera Navis* or Ship of Fools:

> Navigation delivers man to the uncertainty of fate; on water, each of us is in the hands of his own destiny; every embarcation is, potentially, the last. It is for the other world that the madman sets sail in his fool's boat; it is from the other world that he comes when he disembarks. The madman's voyage is at once a rigorous division and an absolute Passage. In one sense, it simply develops, across a half-real, half-imaginary geography, the madman's liminal position. . . . Confined on the ship, from which there is no escape, the madman is delivered to the river with its thousand arms, the sea with its thousand roads. . . . he is the Passenger par excellence: that is, the prisoner of the Passage.[6]

The venerean metonymies of sea foam and feather (or quill) may thus serve also to signify the act of writing itself, the poet's pen tracing its mental voyage on the silent whiteness of the page. Góngora's language is psychagogic, an attempt to form consciousness in and through a reformation of language.

After the turbulent chaos of the storm, a temporary calm ensues:

> Besa la arena, y de la rota nave
> aquella parte poca
> que le expuso en la playa dió a la roca:
> que aun se dejan las peñas
> lisonjear de agradecidas señas. (I, 29-33)

The period carries the idea of a restoration of order in nature. The elements, before "confused," now begin to separate out into their natural environments. The pilgrim's offering of the wood to the rock completes the life cycle which this agent undergoes, beginning with its initial appearance as an "opuesto pino" in line 15, a cycle which is, in a sense, identical to the pilgrim's own adventure as an exile at sea. The wood (Ovid's *pinus*) is first presented in its natural state on land, then as alienated into "leño"–a part of the ship which carries the pilgrim–then as broken away into the "tabla" which the pilgrim rides to land; finally, it is here reintegrated with its source in the element of earth at the base of the shore cliff. By giving the wood to the rock, the pilgrim is paying nature its due; nature, before "condolido" with his plight, is now "lisonjeado."

The movement of restoration and ordering continues into the fifth strophe. Where before the wood and the pilgrim both return to their proper element, now the pilgrim, by wringing out his clothes, returns water to its place as a free element in the atmosphere and the ocean:

> Desnudo el joven, cuanto ya el vestido
> Océano ha bebido
> *restituir le hace* a las arenas;
> y al sol lo extiende luego,
> que, lamiéndole apenas
> su dulce lengua de templado fuego,
> lento lo embiste, y con süave estilo
> la menor onda chupa al menor hilo. (I, 34-41)

The hyperbole reinvokes the initial antithesis of fire and water. The sun, appearing again in the guise of Taurus, "licks" the clothes dry, collaborating now in the restoration. Its destructive force as "mentido robador" metamorphoses into images of pastoral domesticity: "dulce lengua," "templado fuego," "suave estilo." With the pilgrim momentarily naked on the beach, sun and ocean, Venus and Jupiter, seem to hover around the scene like proud parents attending the birth of their child.

In the first three strophes Góngora presents the pilgrim principally as a predicate, a passive object of the elementary chaos which overwhelms him. With the "besa la arena" of the fourth strophe, the predication begins to transpose itself; the landscape becomes the object of the active verbs, the pilgrim the subject. The place of these two "intermediate" strophes (since they take place on the beach, the boundary between sea and land) are to compose the landscape shattered by the storm. Part of this composition depends on the sequence of purposive, ritualistic gestures the pilgrim begins to undertake. These will lead into the difficult ascension of the shore cliff which faces him, the first phase of the pilgrimage on land, the entry of the poem into the pastoral utopia of this first *Soledad*:

> No bien pues de su luz los horizontes
> –que hacían desigual, confusamente
> montes de agua y piélagos de montes–
> desdorados los siente,
> cuando–entregado el mísero extranjero
> en lo que ya del mar redimió fiero–
> entre espinas crepúsculos pisando,
> riscos que aun igualara mal, volando,
> veloz, intrépida ala,
> –menos cansado que confuso–escala. (I, 42-51)

The twilight and the danger of the climb tend to bring back the spiral of confusion. The elements again move in a play of inversions: "montes de agua y piélagos de montes." The terminal "escala" brings up short the extended periphrasis of the period. Like the previous ritualization of the rescue, the active verb here introduces into this wild state of nature a series of evolving representations of architecture, agriculture, sport, music, hunting–the multiple forms of human technique and activity which will make of the *Soledades* a pastoral and piscatory *anthology*. In the final period (52-61), consequently, the whole landscape appears from the summit finally attained as "conquered" and "legislated" by the pilgrim's action:

Vencida al fin la cumbre
–del mar siempre sonante,
de la muda campaña
árbitro igual e inexpugnable muro–,
con pie ya más seguro
declina al vacilante
breve esplendor de mal distinta lumbre:
farol de una cabaña
que sobre el ferro está, en aquel incierto
golfo de sombras anunciando el puerto.

The permutation of elements ("montes de agua") now gives way to distinction: "muda campaña" / "mar sonante." The cliff which marks this distinction acqures an architectonic form ("inexpugnable muro") and an anthropomorphic identity ("árbitro igual"). The central line of "con pie ya más seguro" opposes the earlier "entre espinas crepúsculos pisando" (48) and "una Libia de ondas su camino" (20). With the appearance of the light, the pilgrim's journey will be downwards ("declina") and inland towards its source. This passage, which occupies the rest of the *Soledad primera*, is an anabasis on the "sea" of the land, through mountains, valleys, paths, and orchards, culminating in the haven of the wedding community and the sexual union of the bridal couple.

The "mal distinta lumbre" defines a new process of metamorphosis which ends in the *albergue*, the initial form of a human community which indexes the mastery of consciousness *over* nature:

Llegó pues el mancebo, y saludado,
sin ambición, sin pompa de palabras,
de los conducidores fué de cabras,
que a Vulcano tenían coronado. (90-93)

The "llegó" closes the journey of the pilgrim through the cycle of transformations which had begun in the genetic chaos of the "mentido robador." "Que a Vulcano tenían coronado" (i.e., "surrounding the fire") is the apotheosis of this process. Vulcan is the god of fire and the forge, that is of the purposive subjection of natural energy to the service of human needs and desires. The nocturnal fire which draws the pilgrim away from the wildness of the shore is thus the antithesis of the initial image of the sun as Taurus–fire as a free element, untrammeled energy. Jupiter-Taurus carried the suggestion of psychic and sexual disorder–rape, incest, bestiality, adultery–like Tirso's "burlador," the anarchy of a perpetually shifting identity ("mentido") which threatens to disintegrate the human norm. He is the father, whereas Vulcan is the husband, the sublimation and socialization of sexual instinct. The *albergue*, as the first albeit "primitive" human society of the *Soledades*, foreshadows the prosperous community of the wedding village and the final secular and erotic apotheosis of Góngora's dialectical calculus in the *Soledad primera*.

The "mentido robador" suggests perhaps Cascales' definition of the *Soledades* as a Babel "volviendo a su primer caos las cosas." But we have seen that this crisis of language is ultimately an illusion. The expanding tissue of words reaches a limit of *confusion*, then dissolves into a series of structured *figures* which hold in order the progessive metamorphosis of the signifier. The order of language and the order of life come into a kind of complementarity. This represents a mastery of contradiction and contingency through technique in an historical and ideological world which has become for the poet a "soledad confusa."[7] The pilgrim is ourselves: mind representing its own creative movement in a world constantly transformed by its own activity, mediating the wonder but also the dissonance it encounters in its experience of the world, exercising its resources of memory, desire, and imagination, moving from contemplation to action "paso a paso." Góngora's wager in the *Soledades* is with creating a *possible* language that could begin to express the human condition as a utopian harmony of being and language, work and community, freedom and order, the human and the natural. That is why there is always behind its radiance and sensuality the logic of tragedy, of the disillusion human beings must pass through in order to move forward in their environment. He begins in the half-light of a world of myth, in the sunset of Dürer's allegory of melancholy: "menos cansado que confuso." But the *Soledades* are a language which suggests the form of another world and another beginning. "All mythology subdues, controls and fashions the forces of nature in the imagination and through the imagination; it disappears therefore when real control over these forces is established."[8]

3

Structure as Figure in the "Soledades"

Form conceived as content itself, incessantly changing shape in relation to previous models . . .

Boris Eichenbaum
"The Theory of the Formal Method"

Trescientos sesenta y cinco árboles tiene la selva
Trescientos sesenta y cinco selvas tiene el año
Cuántas se necesitan para formar un siglo
Un niño se perdería en ellas hasta el fin del siglo
Y aprendería el canto de todos los pájaros

Vicente Huidobro
"Ronda de la vida riendo"

Modern editions of the *Soledades* generally obey the format established by Dámaso Alonso in 1927 which divides the poem into semi-strophes or "párrafos."[1] Maurice Molho, however, has argued convincingly that "la division traditionelle des *Soledades* en stances inégales est artificielle. Si elle facilite la lecture, elle masque la nature vraie de la *silva*, dont le propre est d'être une forme a-strophique."[2] The *Obras en verso del Homero español* that Juan de Vicuña prepared in 1627 on the basis of manuscript copies of the poem, for example, does not attempt such divisions but rather renders each of the two cantos as a single *silva*.[3] A glance at any page of this edition will serve to confirm Spitzer's image of the poem as a *Satzlabyrinth* or language labyrinth.

The Vicuña text of the *Soledades* is far from satisfactory in other respects, so that one may suspect a certain editorial anachronism in this method of presenting the poem. I am inclined to think, however, that it reproduces the form in which Góngora intended his *silva* to appear. For one thing, the sheer difficulty of reading page after page of the poem without stanzaic pauses suggests the "vacilando el entendimiento en fuerza del discurso, trabajándole" that Góngora writes about in his letter defending the composition of the *Soledades*. The *silva* as a poetic ideoform derives from Tasso's *Aminta* and the

Italian genre known as *boschereccia*. Molho makes note of a macaronic poem of the sixteenth century titled curiously *Caos del Triperuno in selve tripartito* in which "selve" was meant to signify both the poetic form of each of the three cantos and the "dark wood," as in Dante, of the state of Creation which the poem sought to represent.[4] There is a Virgilian precedent for this sort of thing (and consequently one perhaps closer to Góngora's taste) in the proposition of the fourth *Bucolic* which intimates the return of the Golden Age:

> Sicelides Musae, paulo maiora canamus.
> Non omnes arbusta iuvant humilesque myricae;
> *si canimus silvas, silvae sint consulae dignae.* [Italics added.]

Góngora offers his poem as a "soledad confusa," "soledad" designating among other things a wilderness, the state of nature. Díaz de Rivas spoke of an "obra sylvestre," tugging at the etymological tie of "silva" and "selva."[5] Such images refer to the body of the poem itself, the *silva* which becomes on the page of the text the graphic embodiment of a confusion in which the reader must find his way. Molho elaborates the conceit:

> –d'une parte, la *selva*, paysage naturel, indompté, où la végétation se donne libre cours dans un désordre touffu d'arbres, de plantes, de sources et de fleurs;
>
> –d'autre part, la *silva*, forme a-strophique, dédale de vers inégaux et des rimes enchevêtrées–fôret métrique, exubérante et indisciplinée.
>
> La *silva* et la *selva* sont, l'une et l'autre, un refus de structure. Leur rapport est celui d'une forme métrique et d'une substance poétique congruentes en raison de leur fondamentale identité.[6]

But "refus de structure" is too strong. The *Soledades* are not strictly astrophic; they only *appear* to be. Or, to put this another way, the enveloping, unmarked *silva* is the organic form of each canto, but in its process of development it produces miniatures of itself–Góngora's "tropos"–which the reader can isolate and identify. Natural form is thus both imitated and "read" in the *Soledades*, somewhat in the fashion that Gracián has the wild child, Andrenio, read the mysteries of nature from his island shelter in the *Criticón*:

> . . . percibía acá fuera unas voces como la tuya, *al comenzar con grande confusión y estruendo, pero después poco a poco más distintas* [italics mine], que naturalmente me alborozaban o se me quedaban muy impresas en el ánimo. . . . Una cosa puedo asegurarte: que con que imaginé muchas veces y de mil modos lo que habría acá fuera, el modo, la disposición, la traza, el sitio, la variedad y máquina de cosas, según lo que yo había concebido, jamás di en el modo ni atiné con el orden, variedad y grandeza desta gran fábrica que vemos y admiramos.[7]

I can illustrate the point better by taking a brief look at one aspect of Góngora's poetic exercise: his handling of rhyme pattern in the *Soledades*. The special novelty of Góngora's *silva* is that he uses it for a long narrative. The longest *silva* proper prior to the *Soledades* is Jáuregui's *Acaecimiento amoroso* which totalled only 175 lines. It was the *octava rima*, rather, which was thought prerequisite for the elaboration of epic or a long poem. Its effectiveness in this context derived from the ability of the stanza to coordinate a syntactic period rendered in eight hendecasyllables (or, with a semicolon, in two quartets) with the linking pattern of the ABABABCC rhyme scheme. This gave both the poet and the reader a way of regulating the flow of the lines of verse through a repeated trajectory of expansion and closure (the terminal couplet). Góngora used it in precisely this sense in the *Polifemo* and the *Panegírico*. And it appears in variant forms at times in the *Soledades*. For example, the terminal strophe of the *Soledad primera* is an *octava* in hendecasyllables but rhymed as four couplets AABBCCDD. But what Molho means to suggest in saying the poem is astrophic is that its combination of free alternation in the double meter and varied rhyme pattern does not define any "regular" pattern of repetition like the *octava* or the earlier *silva* strophes of, say, Herrera's *canciones heroicas*. The "Carta de un amigo" spoke of "un cuaderno de versos desiguales y consonancias erráticas" (Millé, Epistolario 127).

The *silva* of 37 lines which makes up the *Dedicatoria* is independent of the main text, so it can serve as a model here. Dámaso Alonso tried to divide it into four periods: the proposition (1-4), the hunt (5-12), the end of the hunt and the *locus amoenus* (13-32), and the terminal dedication (33-37). The reader who has the text before him will note a certain logic in this division; but it does not really fit perfectly with the syntax and, moreover, is countermanded by a rhyme scheme which develops through the lines in a seamless transition: ABBC–DACEDEFF–GHHGCIICJJKLDDKLMCCM–MNNOO. Passing immediately to the opening section of the *Soledad primera* (1-33, that is, up to the point the pilgrim reaches land), one can observe a similar process: ABCDDEBACEFGFG–HIIJHHJ–FKKLLFM–MNNOO. Again, Alonso's "párrafos" are partially eroded by the constant introduction of new rhymes and the repetition at intervals of previously established ones. The rhyme expansion in both cases reaches a limit and terminates in a cascade of couplets (MMNNOO).

A more complex case is presented by lines 182-222 of the *Soledad primera* which describe the pilgrim's departure from the shepherds and his meditation on some nearby ruins and the river. Dámaso Alonso's edition renders the whole sequence as four strophes: (1) 182-89 (the departure), (2) 190-93 (the overlook), (3) 194-211 (meditation on the river), (4) 212-21 (elegy on the ruins). Góngora molds these lines up to the end of the ecphrasis (211) as a series of independently rhymed quartets: (1) ABBA CDDC (a tacit *octava*); (2) AABB; then, in the ecphrasis itself, (3) ABAB CDDC (a tacit *octava* ending with the semicolon after "útilmente"), ABBA CDDC, and a terminal couplet. At first the quartet schemes fit the syntactic flow. The terminal rhyme of the first quartet of the ecphrasis, however, belongs with the new sentence beginning "Muda la admiración, habla call*ando*" (197). The asymmetry between strophe and syntax thus created is partially resolved in the firm rhyme of the couplet at the end: "adonde"/"esconde." (4) But in the subsequent elegy the quartet pattern breaks up entirely into an ABCCABDDEE. After the couplet of the elegy, the rhyme scheme spirals away in the manner of the *Dedicatoria*, mimicking the sudden motion and noise of the hunting party—"*torrente* de armas y de perros"—which interrupts the melancholy meditations (222-32).

This apparent anarchy of rhyme produces a "confusion," but like the scenes it represents a "sweet confusion," the pleasure of being momentarily in an undetermined space. The reader, like the pilgrim, is never lost for long because the *silva* is a territory of language which is constantly "mapping" itself as it passes before the spectator. The poem is built around the spatial figure of the *soledad* as a natural and psychic wilderness. Like Marvell's *Garden*, this is a case where language creates a *nature* in order to escape from the alienating reason of its experience of the world. But this escape is also a way of creating a new order of perception, a freer and more harmonious mediation of perception and reality. Góngora invites the reader to work with him in the construction of the poem. The lines of verse are like the footsteps of someone lost in a wilderness; but they are also the ongoing path of a pilgrimage: the labor of the reader's intelligence and persistence.

The first *soledad* is formed as a bucolic anabasis, a comedy ending in the ritual of the wedding; the second is a piscatory poem ending as a tragedy in the intimation of a "bride" (Persephone) consigned to darkness and death. This binary structure of two cantos conceals a tacit four part division of the poem forced by Góngora's recourse to the period of a day as his basic unit of time. It will be objected that the action of the *Soledades* unfolds over *five* days. But the first and fifth (that is, the opening and closing parts of the poem) are only fragments of the period of a day, whereas the second, third, and fourth are complete, both as units of time and of action. The reader is to intuit that the first and last days, taken together, form the unit of a "fourth" complete period of a day in an inverted relationship of beginning and end. The first begins in what is apparently the late afternoon ("campos de zafiro") and ends at night with the pilgrim sleeping in the *albergue*; the last begins at dawn and ends with the retirement of the hawking party along the shore. The image of the owl's wing blotting out the sunlight and the exhaustion of the party evidently suggest the late afternoon and the approach of darkness (II, 975).

Each of these periods of a day will organize the action of the poem into *distinct* spatial-temporal units underneath the graphic fiction of the *silva*. The first canto covers two and a half periods of a day, the second one and a half as follows:

(1) First whole period of a day: lines 176-700 of the *Soledad primera* (624 lines). This describes the pilgrim's Arcadian anabasis down the mountainside along a stream with the shepherds and *serranos* who are going to the wedding. It ends with their evening celebration which takes place on the outskirts of the wedding village.

(2) Second period of a day: I, 701 to end (390 lines). This describes the village wedding in the manner of the Baroque *comedia* blended with Virgil. The pilgrim enters the village, hears a hymeneal song set for alternate choruses of men and women, attends a wedding banquet capped by a prudential speech by the bride's father, enjoys with the guests afternoon games in which the villagers compete with the mountain folk, and finally joins the retirement in the evening of the wedding party to their homes and lodgings and the bridal couple to their wedding bed: "los novios entra en dura no estacada."

(3) Third period of a day: beginning to line 676 of the *Soledad segunda* (676 lines). This describes the pilgrim's visit with a family on an island off the coast he reaches on the morning following the wedding. I will deal with it in more detail below.

(4) Fourth period of a day (combining, that is, the nominal first and fifth days of the story): lines 1-175 of the *Soledad primera*, 677 to end of the *Soledad segunda* (477 lines). This day is formed, as noted, by the conceited identity of beginning and ending. Its "dawn" is in the second canto, its "sunset" in the first. The initial wilderness and steep shore cliff metamorphose into a "desigualdad del horizonte, / que deja de ser monte / por ser culta floresta" (II, 692-94), the rustic *albergue* into a marble palace, the goatherds into the prince and his retinue of hawkers. In both, the topic of place, however, is essentially the same: Góngora's "la incierta ribera."

The beginning of each of these periods of a day will be structurally marked by an invocation of the dawn and sunrise: (1) I, 176-89, as the pilgrim leaves the *albergue*; (2) I, 705-21, as he enters the wedding village; (3) II, 26-41, as he embarks with a group of guests departing from the wedding; (4) II, 676-85, as he leaves the island where he was entertained by the old fisherman and his family. These invocations form a mnemonic chain in which the details of one are echoed and transformed in the others. Note, for example, the counterpoint of mood and figures between the mountain sunrise which greets the pilgrim in the *albergue* and the valley sunrise which announces the day of the wedding:

. . . las aves
–esquilas dulces de sonora pluma–
señas dieron süaves
del alba al Sol, que el pabellón de espuma
dejó, y en su carroza
rayó el verde obelisco de la choza. (I, 176-81)

Recordó al Sol, *no*, de su espuma cana,
la dulce de las aves armonía,
sino los dos topacios que batía
–orientales aldabas–Himeneo.
Del carro, pues, febeo
el luminoso tiro,
mordiendo oro, el eclíptico zafiro
pisar quería, cuando . . . [etc.] (I, 705-12)

The piscatory sunrise which opens the *Soledad segunda* and the third period of a day yields:

Ruiseñor *en los bosques* no más blando,
el verde robre que es barquillo ahora,
saludar vió la Aurora,
que al uno en dulces quejas–y no pocas–
ondas endurecer, liquidar rocas. (II, 37-41)

The topic of the chariot of Phoebus and its horses, introduced in the two dawns of the first *Soledad*, reappears in the invocation of the final day as:

Las horas ya, de números vestidas,
al bayo, cuando no esplendor overo
del luminoso tiro, las pendientes
ponían de crisólitos lucientes,
coyundas impedidas (II, 677-81)

The team, before "mordiendo" now "impedidas," are in turn reflected by the Andalusian stallion of the prince which the pilgrim watches from his rowboat (with "bayos" and "overos" curiously inverted):

que a mucho humo abriendo
la fogosa nariz, en un sonoro
relincho y otro saludó sus rayos.
Los overos, si no esplendores bayos,
que conducen el día,
les responden, la eclíptica ascendiendo. (II, 729-34)

The other term of the period of a day, sunset and evening, is marked correspondingly by the following passages: (1) I, 630-51, a twilight dilated by the fireworks of the prewedding festival; (2) I, 1062-72, ending the games with the retirement of the guests and the bridal couple; (3) II, 512-30, ending the dinner on the island and introducing the twilight eclogue of two fishermen; (4) I, 41-51, the metamorphoses of the "mal distinta lumbre" we considered in Chapter 1. Each day then passes into an epilogue, an invitation to night and sleep: (1) I, 163-79, after the excesses of the festival; (2) I, 1084-91, the ending *octava* of the *Soledad primera* with its suggestion of the "dura no estacada" of the lovers after the exertions of the games; (3) II, 652-76, in the form of a paean to Cupid celebrating the reconciliation of the fishermen with the daughters of the old fisherman of the island; (4) I, 163-76, as the pilgrim falls asleep in the *albergue* after the dangers he passes through in the first part of his story. Where the sunrise passages invoke the image of Phoebus as virile strength and daring, these night pieces resonate with the sheltering and erotic presence of Venus: "le solicitan pieles blandas," "esquilas dulces de sonora pluma," "señas dieron suaves," "a revelar secretos," "de las plumas que baten más suaves," "cuán dulces te adjudicas," and so forth. Góngora is fond of passing immediately from the invitation to sleep to the description of the awakening sunrise which recommences the pilgrimage. The bird song of the *albergue* night, for example, appears inside the pilgrim's pleasant reverie but also *outside* as the sign of morning which awakens him: "Durmió, y *recuerda al fin*, cuando las aves . . ." (I, 176-81). This sort of effect, like the fireworks of I, 630-51, blurs the precise delimitation of the period of a day and dissolves it as a structural unit back into the diachronic flux of the *silva*.

The period of a day is the exemplary unit of time of the pastoral, the figure which mirrors the reconciliation of an alienated consciousness. The epitome of the figure in the Spanish Renaissance was Garcilaso's framing of the *Egloga primera* within a sunrise exordium and a sunset epilogue which begin and close the "quejas" of Salicio and Nemoroso:

> . . . y recordando
> ambos como de sueño, y acabando
> el fugitivo sol, de luz escaso,
> su ganado llevando,
> se fueron recogiendo paso a paso.

But Góngora is also close to the sense the figure acquires in Baroque didactic allegory as the representation of the span of human life and history, the time of *vanitas*. Calderón: the roses which open their buds to the morning sunrise close upon themselves in the embrace of night; like mighty nations "cuna y sepulcro en un botón hallaron" (*El príncipe constante*, Act II, Scene xiv). This calculus of mortality will give way in the rationalist poetics of the eighteenth century to the association of the period of a day as in the prescribed unit of dramatic time with the representation of the process of a social and sentimental *enlightenment*.[8] By joining both ends of the *Soledades* into a single period of a day, Góngora seems to be establishing the temporal form as a meta-figure of the whole poem, which is then like a "day" beginning with the luminosity of the opening scenes and ending abruptly as the owl's wing eclipses the sun in the final lines of the *Soledad segunda*. The *Soledades* are a being of light, but it is a light which is modeled by night and dream.

Within the trajectory of each period of a day, Góngora joins his marking of the passage of the hours with the spatial movement of his pilgrim through the constantly changing variety of landscape and human community:

> Viendo, pues, que igualmente les quedaba
> para el lugar a ellas de camino
> lo que al Sol para el lóbrego occidente (I, 630-33)

The pilgrim, like the *silva*, seems to be compelled to perpetual movement and transformation, the contiguity of a "libertad, de fortuna perseguida." This is balanced, however, by moments in which he is brought to rest—"impedido"—while he witnesses some spectacle in nature or listens to someone else speaking. The effect of this pattern of stopping and resumption of movement in the poem is to compose within the *silva* and the period of a day a series of internally complete subpoems, each reflecting a particular type of form and expression. Placing the story aside, the *Soledades* can be read simply as an anthology of Renaissance poetic form: the Horatian encomium of the "Bienaventurado albergue," a brief elegy on the theme of ruins (I, 212-21), an imitation of Catullus' hymeneal choruses (I, 767-844), a miniature epic in the *Soledad primera* and a mock epic (the fisherman's tale) in the *Soledad segunda*, the pilgrim's piscatory soliloquy (II, 116-71) and the responding alternate eclogue of the two fishermen (II, 542-611), a paean to Cupid (II, 652-76), variations on the Pindaric victory ode in the wedding games and the hawking. At this level of division we arrive close to the structural pseudostrophes Dámaso Alonso carved out of the text. Rather than a refusal of structure, as Molho argues, the *Soledades* display an "uncertain" structure which is meant to appear and disappear as the reader moves back and forth between the *silva* as a metrical-natural labyrinth and as a landscape which is always mapping and formalizing itself. Góngora wants to render the Lucretian vision of a world in ceaseless development. That is part of the realism of the *Soledades*, the pressure of history on the poet's exercise of form. At the same time, he wants to *compose* this process, to render its law of motion.

A consideration of the third period of a day (II, 1-676) may serve to detail this double articulation of form. In the early dawn, the pilgrim finds himself again on the shoreline, about to embark with a group of the guests from the wedding on two fishing boats which appear with the sunrise. He departs with two brothers and spends the morning helping them with their fishing in what is apparently an estuary. After confiding to the water a painful soliloquy on his exile, he disembarks on an island where he is greeted by the father of the fishermen and his six daughters. The pilgrim spends the day touring the island. In the evening he listens to a story recounting the dangers faced by two of the daughters who venture out to hunt large fish. Sunset brings an alternate eclogue by two young fishermen who are in love with the daughters but unable to marry them. The pilgrim intervenes in their behalf with the father, and a paean to Cupid in Góngora's own voice follows, closing the period of a day.

This third day of the *Soledades* divides into a number of subsections defined by Góngora's marking of temporal stages within the period of a day:

(1) II, 1-33. A prelude describing in the light of early dawn the shoreline and the movement of tide and stream in the estuary. It culminates in the appearance of the pilgrim and the wedding party.

(2) II, 34-208. The fishing scenes. These begin with the invocation of sunrise and occupy the "morning" of this day. They include the pilgrim's soliloquy (112-71) and end in the arrival of the fishing skiff at the island.

(3) II, 208-511. The "afternoon" section. It encloses two major subepisodes: the tour the pilgrim and his host make of the island (248-346) which ends in a dinner along the shore and the piscatory tale of the old fisherman (388-511).

(4) II, 512-676. The "evening" scenes, or the amoeban eclogue, the pilgrim's intervention in this "querella de amor," and the concluding paean to Cupid.

Where, at the start of the *Soledad primera*, the pilgrim is moving from the chaos of the sea to the shoreline and, after his arrival, will proceed inland towards the *albergue* as night falls, here he appears with the sunrise on the shoreline, his anabasis terminated in the wedding, preparing to embark once again. The first strophe of the prelude, consequently, describes the outlet of a stream descended from the same mountains through which the pilgrim had walked with the band of shepherds:

> Entrase el mar por un arroyo breve
> que a recibillo con sediento paso
> de su roca natal se precipita,
> y mucha sal no sólo en poco vaso,
> mas su rüina bebe,
> y su fin, cristalina mariposa
> –no alada, sino undosa–,
> en el farol de Tetis solicita. (II, 1-8)

Compare the terminal lines of the vision of the river from the mountainside in the *Soledad primera*:

rocas abraza, islas aprisiona,
de la alta gruta donde se desata
hasta los jaspes líquidos, adonde
su orgullo pierde y su memoria esconde. (I, 208-11)

The image of the stream as a butterfly attracted to its death in the "farol de Tetis" of the sea recalls the end of the series of metaphoric variations on the "breve luz" which guides the pilgrim to the *albergue*:

y la que desviada
luz poca pareció, tanta es vecina,
que yace en ella la robusta encina,
mariposa en cenizas desatada. (I, 86-89)

The epitaphic conceit there depended on the identity of the flames of the burning log with the wings of the butterfly achieved through the "moths to fire" *topos*. Its underlying logic is the order of transition between the material elements–earth to fire to air. Here, instead, we are given a "cristalina mariposa," the identity now suggested by the ripples and waves of its course–water to air to earth: the opposition of fluid and fixed. Both emblematize the idea of nature as a providential cycle in which the end of something is necessarily contingent with the birth of something else.

The interaction of land and ocean along the "incierta ribera" in the early light which precedes the sunrise is "confused" in the same way as the details of the evening landscape of the shipwreck. The beach standing against the force of the incoming tide is like a "novillo tierno" in struggle with a "duro toro"– the sea is "hard," the land "soft." The image of the bull had been introduced above the shipwreck as "y el sol todos los rayos de su pelo"–the free play of cosmic force. It was then metamorphosed or "adapted" to domestic utility in the image of the sun-bull licking dry the pilgrim's clothes on the beach. Now it is the ocean as "centauro ya espumoso" which violates the land like the "mentido robador," forming an inlet which is "medio mar, medio ría." To define the conjunction of sun and moon in the late afternoon sky, Góngora had added to his Jupiter-Taurus "media luna las armas de su frente"; here the tideland of the inlet appears as a ". . . novillo tierno, / de bien nacido cuerno / mal lunada la frente" and "dos cuernos del mar." (The pilgrim is a young man–a "mancebo"–whose rashness is being constantly compared with and mediated by the wise disillusion of the elders he meets in the poem.)

Lines 22 to 26 of the respective cantos are coded in almost exact parallelism:

I Del Océano pues antes sorbido,
y luego vomitado
no lejos de un escollo *coronado*

de secos juncos, de calientes plumas,
–alga todo y espumas–

II no pues de otra manera
a la violencia mucha
del padre de las aguas, *coronado*
de blancas ovas y de espuma verde,
resiste obedeciendo, y tierra pierde.

Where in the *Soledad primera* (as a *pastoral* invention) the pilgrim leaves the sea and gains the land, in this prelude of the *piscatory Soledad segunda* the sea covers the land and the pilgrim prepares to reembark. Both passages resonate in turn with the ending octave of the first canto with its evocation of the bed of white feathers Venus has prepared for the bridal couple who are to enter, in contrast to the "desigual lucha" of land and tide, a "dura no estacada." Góngora rarely misses in his poetry the opportunity to suggest an erotic allegory. He carries over the expectation of the love-making of the bridal couple into the interplay of liquid and solid in this prelude of the "next day":

Entrase el mar por un arroyo breve
que a recibillo con sediento paso
de su roca natal se precipita (II, 1-3)

The effect also serves to mediate the structural transition between the two cantos; Góngora "couples" them, as it were, making the end of the first contiguous in part with the beginning of the second in much the same way as he joins the two outer days of the poem–the first and the fifth–into a single period of a day. It is interesting to note too that the images of the ending section of the *Soledad segunda*–especially the shoreline huts "de las ondas no menos / aquéllos perdonados / que de la tierra éstos admitidos" (II, 951-53)–reproduce the characteristic blurring of the boundary between land and water, light and darkness, in the opening sections of the two parts.

Up to this point in the third period of a day, we have been dealing with a world of pure matter and energy portrayed in the predawn transition between night and day without the presence of a human protagonist. With the sunrise (line 33), the pilgrim and the wedding party appear, having come from the village of the previous day to the beach where they will return by boat to their homes. Two fishing skiffs approach to meet them. Over the water, they hear from one of the skiffs fragments of "dulces quejas" that the fishermen are singing, which seem (again the blurring of land and water) to "harden" the waves, "liquify" the rocks (41).

The fishing scenes which follow betray Góngora's ambition to make the *Soledades*, among other things, a Hispano-Andalusian *Georgics*. They tally with, for example, the celebration of agriculture in the epithalamium, the games of the wedding, the hawking scenes of the final day, and the action of the two stories interpolated in the poem–the miniature nautical epic in the first *Soledad*, the fisherman's tale in the second. The place of the pilgrim's Horatian (and conventionally bucolic) encomium in the *albergue* (I, 95-135) is now taken by a piscatory soliloquy which is set against the labor of the fishing (II, 112-71). This is a more deeply subjective statement than the earlier intimation of corruption and failure in the "moderno artificio" of the Court, as if the incomplete hero, like Don Quijote, had come to a new vision of his life and destiny through the spiraling anabasis of the *Soledad primera*:

> "Esta, pues, culpa mía
> el timón alternar menos seguro
> y el báculo más duro
> un lustro ha hecho a mi dudosa mano,
> solicitando en vano
> las alas sepultar de mi osadía
> donde el sol nace o donde muere el día." (II, 144-50)

The meditation into the riddle of his character is borne away by the sea and the wind before it can be finished. The boat approaches the island. Góngora neatly transits to the disembarcation and the beginning of the third, or afternoon, section of the period of a day around a syntactically forced caesura:

> Lo que agradable más se determina
> del breve islote, ocupa su fortuna,
> los extremos de fausto y de miseria
> moderando.
>
> En la plancha los recibe
> el padre de los dos . . . (205-09)

This section again lends itself to a division into four episodes: (1) the presentation (208-47), (2) the tour (247-336), (3) the dinner (337-87), and, as evening approaches, (4) the tale (388-511). I want to consider in some detail the tour, since it serves as a model for understanding the way in which Góngora plays action against structural marking. After greeting the pilgrim, the host sends his daughters to prepare a meal for him. They disappear, and the two men begin an excursion around the island. Some 80 lines further along, this peripatetic will end in a grove formed by six poplar trees which becomes, transitively, the site of the dinner served by the daughters, who now reappear.

The tour resembles in its development the spectacle of the parade of gifts brought to the wedding (I, 267-355), the procession of the hawking party (II, 713-830), and, in a different way, the descriptive ecphrasis on the river (I, 194-211). Góngora's manner in these episodes derives from the Classical device of periphrastic amplification: the Shield of Achilles which reveals a plethora of potential fictions and landscapes. The tour is a "passage," but it interrupts the general movement of the pilgrim through the geography of the poem by containing him on the island. In the case of the parade of gifts, Góngora has him literally embedded in a hollow trunk from which he views the scene (I, 267-68) and which he abandons some 80 lines later ("Menos en renunciar tardó la encina"–350) to join the parade. The tour and its analogues, that is, are moments of discourse, complete within themselves but framed lexically by the pilgrim's acts of stopping and recommencing his journey in the "pasos-versos" movement of the *silva*. They are dilations of a *time of observation* which is necessary to prepare the pilgrim and the reader to undertake their movement forward in the text; in this sense, they miniaturize the dynamics of the whole poem.

Throughout these second and third parts of the third period of a day, Góngora is concerned with portraying the small island community of the fisherman as a distillation of all the natural abundance and variety of the *Soledad primera*. The island, as noted above, emblematizes the pastoral ideal of *mediocritas*:

> Estimando seguía el peregrino
> al venerable isleño,
> *de muchos pocos* numeroso dueño (314-16)
>
> en breve espacio mucha primavera (339)
>
> Lo que agradable más se determina
> del breve islote, ocupa su fortuna,
> *los extremos de fausto y de miseria*
> moderando. (205-08)
>
> Del pobre albergue a la barquilla pobre,
> *geómetra prudente*, el orbe mida
> vuestra planta, impedida (380-82)

In the tour the pilgrim is actually moving in space, but the "breve islote" defines a "prudent" *enclosure*. The same effect of an isolated but complete world makes the island, for example, a common scenographic setting in utopian fictions. The tour is framed by our awareness that it commences sometime in the morning after the fishing and ends in the poplar grove in late afternoon with the dinner. As in Garcilaso's pastoral the flow of time is placed "in parenthesis." The pilgrim is a man lost in history, compelled to move beyond the rhythm of nature. He fears the possibility of a "fin duro a mi destierro" in the soliloquy. The invitation confines him for a moment, restores his contact with an experience that is other than his perception of time as a tragic fate: "*Impidiéndole el día* al forastero" (II, 248).

The tour is structured as a *round* which emblematizes the cycle of creation and destruction in nature. It encloses seven distinct scenes:

(1) The swans (248-62). A scene set on the shoreline where the swans nest and the tour commences. Góngora sets up a color chromatics which he will vary and transform in each of the succeeding scenes:

> entre unos verdes carrizales, donde
> armonïoso número se esconde
> de blancos cisnes . . .

The contrast of green and white unfolds into a brief drama of the life cycle of the swan. The dry rushes of the shore "vivify" the swan's eggs. In the same place a swan is dying. Her song echoes the piscatory soliloquy of the pilgrim. Another leads her children to the sea:

> y mientras dulce aquél su muerte anuncia
> entre la verde juncia,
> sus pollos éste al mar conduce nuevos,
> de Espío y de Nerea
> –cuando más obscurecen las espumas–
> nevada invidia, sus nevadas plumas.

The expected *topos* is, of course, "black envy." The piscatory numphs, whose white skin "obscures" the white of the sea foam, envy the virgin white feathers of the young swans. The simultaneity of birth and death represents the chain of natural providence (Venus' symbols in the poem are "espuma" and "pluma.") What nature takes away it restores in the form of new life; the old makes way for the new.

(2) The doves (263-74). This scene opens with a mythic allusion to "alamo" or *white* poplar ("junco" in the seventh scene is a *black* poplar): "Hermana de Faetón, verde el cabello." The reader of Ovid knows Phaeton's sister is metamorphosed into this tree. Here the fisherman had constructed when he was young ("ya gallardo") a dovecote which becomes allusively a temple of Venus: "donde celosa arrulla y ronca gime / la ave lasciva de la cipria diosa." Góngora conflates the dovecote with the lookout of a warship: "Mástiles coronó menos crecidos, / gavia no tan capaz . . ." as if to contrast this realm of pastoral fecundity with an image of epic.

(3) The rabbits (275-82). The rabbits are on a hillock garlanded with laurel trees ("las sienes laureado") whose "confusos senos" form their breeding ground, a natural hutch.

(4) The bees (283-301). This is the most complex of the scenes. The beehive is in a "cóncavo fresno" or hollow ash (compare "De una encina embebido / en lo cóncavo . . ." in the *Soledad primera*). The space of the hollow trunk is the

site of the "republic of bees"–Carthage, given the equation of the queen bee with "Dido alada." A whole urban universe in miniature within the already miniaturized universe of the "breve islote" appears:

> verde era pompa de un vallete oculto,
> cuando frondoso alcázar no, de aquella,
> que sin corona vuela y sin espada,
> susurrante amazona, Dido alada,
> de ejército más casto, de más bella
> república, ceñida, en vez de muros,
> de cortezas; en esta, pues, Cartago
> reina la abeja, oro brillando vago,
> o el jugo beba de los aires puros,
> o el sudor de los cielos, cuando liba
> de las mudas estrellas la saliva;
> burgo eran suyo el tronco informe, el breve
> corcho, y moradas pobres sus vacíos,
> del que más solicita los desvíos
> de la isla, plebeyo enjambre leve.

(5) The goats (303-13). Since the goats are upon a promontory which is the highest point on the island, they are "estrellado" on their pasture ground. As "stars," they invoke their astrological archetype, the constellation of Capricorn which is commonly considered the zenith of the zodiac:

> de cabras *estrellado*,
> iguales, aunque pocas,
> a la que–imagen décima del cielo–
> flores su cuerno es, *rayos su pelo*.

The image links with Góngora's use of the constellation of Taurus as a zodiacal sign of spring in the opening of the *Soledad primera* ("cuerno"/"media luna," "rayos su pelo"/"los rayos de su pelo," "estrellado"/"pace estrellas"):

> –*media luna* las armas de su frente,
> y el Sol todos *los rayos de su pelo*–,
> luciente honor del cielo,
> en campos de zafiro pace estrellas (I, 3-6)

The "flores su cuerno es" inverts the conceit in the preceding scene of bees sipping "las mudas estrellas." The goats complete the cycle of animals–swan, dove, rabbit, bee–emblematic of natural fecundity. ("Tres o cuatro desean para ciento," notes the fisherman.) Hence, perhaps, their connection with Jupiter as "mentido robador" in the sexual myth which opens the poem.

(6) The spring (314-27). In the convention of the *locus amoenus*, the spring

is the symbol of the source of nature ("... o de la fuente / la alta cenefa ..." in the dedication). Góngora presents the flowing water as intertwined with the roots of a pine tree, the figure of a "trodden snake" ("—aljófar vomitando fugitivo / en lugar de veneno—") which in its writhing composes a miniature Arcadian landscape:

> torcida esconde, ya que no enroscada,
> las flores, que de un parto dió lascivo
> aura fecunda al matizado seno
> del huerto, en cuyos troncos se desata
> de las escamas que vistió de plata

(7) The black poplars (328-36). The variations on white, green, and black and their harmonics (for example, the "aljófar" of the spring) culminate in the contrast of six black-barked poplars intertwined by coils of ivy with an "encanecido suelo de lilios." They form allusively the sacred glade of Dionysius: "tirsos eran del griego dios, nacido / segunda vez...." The invocation is meant to pick up the life cycle of the swan depicted in the first unit and to summarize the major theme of the tour: the reproductive fertility of nature. Dionysius indexes the cycle of birth, growth, maturation, death (or harvest), and resurrection of the agricultural year: "nevó el mayo, a pesar de los seis chopos."

The intricate detail of the tour serves to illustrate Góngora's tendency in the *Soledades* to a narrative or descriptive amplification of his material which seems to dilate its containing structures, "pidiendo términos disformes." The unit against which the natural cornucopia is posed is the island; hence the norm of *mediocritas*: "de muchos pocos dueño." We are here, as everywhere in the poem, in the presence of a creative movement of language which has to struggle to keep itself within an order of intelligence and beauty. The pilgrim passes from the world of an intimate nature described in the tour to the mock epic drama of the two daughters who hunt large fish on the sea with which the host entertains him after the dinner. This story, again, in the character or furor of its subject—the dangers of hunting, the girls as piscatory amazons—seems to explode the "prudent" limits of the island world. But the story is strategically interrupted by the light breeze which comes over the sea at sunset, as if to suggest that nature, disturbed by the extremity of the human drama, moves to carry it away and to restore its own order of succession:

> Aura en esto marina
> *el discurso, y el día juntamente,*
> trémula, si veloz, les arrebata (512-14)

The "arrebatamiento" reintroduces the time marking of the period of a day which had been suspended during the course of the story. The miniature naval epic about the Conquest in the *Soledad primera* is broken off in much the same way:

> En suspiros con esto,
> y en más *anegó* lágrimas *el resto*
> *de su discurso* el montañés *prolijo*,
> que el viento su caudal, el mar su hijo. (I, 503-06)

I noted, in studying earlier in this chapter Góngora's patterning of rhyme, the "torrente de armas y de perros" of a hunting party which interrupts the prolix meditations on the river and the ruins and puts the pilgrim in motion again. The elegy, consequently, is remembered by the pilgrim as a *fragment* ("Culto *principio* dió al discurso") mediated like its subject through an apparent interaction of human artifice and the fortuitous action of natural accident which draws the observer back into life and the possiblitiy of new experience.

In the *Soledades*, nature is the Lucretian fiction of a mediating Venus who stands behind the poet's own labor of writing. These images of moments of discourse interrupted by or absorbed into nature are distillations of the aesthetics which underlie the poem. They illustrate Góngora's concern with inviting on the order of his form and that which it represents a collaboration between the possibilities of creation, the capacity for *technē*, and the world which surrounds and contains this activity: a new order of consciousness which is defined by neither a perversion of the natural through tragic excess (the drama of the Court and the empire) nor the genetic wilderness of a pure state of nature.[9]

The last section of this period of a day, the night announced by the "aura marina" of sunset, is meant to show the terms of this collaboration brought to bear on an unexpected disharmony in the social world of the island community. It introduces the laments of Micón and Lĭcidas, who complain from their boats of their rejection by two of the old fisherman's daughters. Their alternate piscatory eclogue summarizes the tone of vague melancholy which hovers over the activities and scenes of this day. The pilgrim, for the first and only time in the *Soledades*, leaves his character as a passive observer and intervenes to have his host grant the marriage the fishermen request.

Spitzer saw the wedding which forms the apotheosis of the *Soledad primera* as emerging out of a geometric texture of antithesis and binary alternation.[10] This was a way of representing the internal tensions and contradictions of the material Góngora handles there, brought finally to a partial perception of conjuncture and identity. But we have seen that the third period of a day begins with and carries over the image of a "soledad confusa" as a binary labyrinth. The language of the prelude which describes the interaction of land and tide establishes the presence of an antithetical reality: "centauro," "medio mar, medio rĭa," "novillo tierno" versus "duro toro." The pilgrim abandons the wedding guests to take the smaller of the two fishing boats that appear, which "las ondas escarchando vuela" while the larger "con perezoso movimiento / el mar encuentra." The theme of division carries through the ambivalent, sentimental terms of the soliloquy to the description of the huts of the island:

> Dos son las chozas, pobre su artificio
> más aún que caduca su materia:
> de los mancebos dos, la mayor, cuna;
> de las redes la otra y su ejercicio,
> competente oficina. (200-04)

The host as a "viejo Nereo" is father of not only the two boys who ferry the pilgrim to the island but also of the six daughters: "[el] sol en seis luceros dividido." When the pilgrim arrives, they are split into two groups of three, one which is weaving cloth (in, we presume, the "cuna" hut, since this is a domestic industry), the other repairing the nets (in the "oficina"). The allusion to Dionysius which summarizes the trajectory of the tour is to "[el] griego dios, nacido segunda vez." The proposition of the fisherman's tale, since it concerns a pair of the daughters who venture away from the island, alludes in a binary inversion of pastoral and piscatory contexts to Thetis and Diana:

> Tal vez desde los muros destas rocas
> cazar a Tetis veo
> y pescar a Diana en dos barquillas:
> náuticas venatorias maravillas
> de mis hijas oirás, *ambiguo coro* (418-22)

The "amebeo alterno coro" of Micón and Lĭcidas concerns a second pair of daughters:

> dulcĭsimas querellas
> de pescadores dos, de dos amantes
> en redes ambos y en edad iguales.
> Dividiendo cristales,
> en la mitad de un óvalo de plata,
> . . . (516-20)

The pilgrim, who bears his own tragic division from the "enemiga amada," has a fraternal identity with the sentimental plight of the lovers which both allows and impels him to serve as a mediator of their "quejas." The period of a day ends in the paean to Cupid (652-76) which represents, as does the wedding, a movement of *union*:

> ¡Vuela, rapaz, y plumas dando a quejas,
> *los dos reduce al uno* y otro leño,
> mientras perdona tu rigor al sueño! (674-76)

This is merely the skeleton of the constant mathematization of the details of this period of a day in the *Soledades*. Góngora's fascination with the idea of number ("de muchos pocos numeroso dueño") makes the limited world of the island appear to be a potentially infinite texture of alternating perceptions. The profusion is "confusing" but at the same time contains its own internal logic and order. To borrow Gérard Genette's genial aphorism on Baroque poetics, "Le monde ainsi biseauté devient à la fois vertigineux et maniable. . . . *Diviser* (partager) *pour unir*, c'est la formule de l'ordre baroque. N'est-ce pas celle du langage même?"[11]

. . .

The analysis of the composition of the third period of a day above was meant to show the way in which Góngora moves in the *Soledades* between the "unmapped" *silva* in which language appears in the image of the disordered variety of natural spectacle and language as *technique*, a method of assimilating reality to human utility. In this process the form of the *silva* and its content come into a kind of identity. It is not just nature that the *Soledades* present but nature mediated and transformed by history. The language of the poem is continually recovering moments it has occupied in the past as it moves forward; as in Hegel's definition of the historical imagination, it has been invested with the faculty of memory and, hence, of self-consciousness.

Dámaso Alonso divided the material of this period of a day into some 80 distinct strophic/units. Góngora's handling of binary alternation illustrates the algebraic mode involved in the structural patterning of the *Soledades*: a multiplication by division. Given a unity in Aristotle's sense of a contingent and necessary relation of beginning, middle, and end—the bucolic paradigm of the period of a day—Góngora's elaboration yields four subsections (predawn, morning, afternoon, evening), in turn a multitude of distinct episodes, scenes, and their consequent poetic or rhetorical paradigms. The "silva-selva-soledad" equation implies that the reading of the *Soledades* involves the experience of a tactical *destructuring*—the text as a "confusion" of representation. Góngora delights in amplifying structural and thematic episodes by proliferating combinations beyond the apparent unit of enclosure: the miniature epic (exploitation of open space, geographic limit), the fireworks display of the second day (dilation of the normal terms of the period of a day), the island itself, the "Carthage" in the hollow ash tree (multiplication of a limited space). But as in the semantic problem of catachresis considered earlier, there is also an ultimate containing limit. This opposition of contingency and structural order is a response to the problem basic to the theme of the poem: the generation of a recreational space—the whole time of *otium* in which the discourse of the *Soledades* sustains its being. For Góngora the movement of the sentence represents in nuclear form the movement of the text as a whole unit: canonically, the opposition of onset and closure of discourse, exordium, and epilogue. The Pindaric sentence of the *Dedicatoria*, which negotiates 27 lines from " ¡Oh tú, de venablos *impedido*" to "que sus errantes pasos ha votado / a la real *cadena* de tu escudo," constitutes the longest syntactic unit in the *Soledades*. It is this sentence which figures the time of the poem, the period of rest asked of the duke from the fury of the hunt in which the Orphic "instrumento" presents itself: "y, *en cuanto* da el sólicito montero . . . déjate *un rato* hallar del pie acertado." The "en cuanto" defines the tentativeness of the poem as idyl of language. Góngora creates in the *silva* a "libertad, de fortuna perseguida." The image of the duke "impeded" from the hunt must give way to the image of the poem finally "enchained" on the historical (and epic) emblem of the shield. In the conjuncture of the first and last days of the poem, Góngora preserves the pastoral paradigm of poetic *otium*; but he is also able to *dilate* this paradigm into the four complete periods of a day covered by the "errantes pasos." The point is to create a time and space of recovery, a new order in which the oppositions of the dedication (violence/peace, ruler/artist, history/poetry) can be mediated and reconciled. In this sense (and this will be the burden of the discussion that follows), the aesthetic labor of generating a new poetic form in the *Soledades* is also an *ideological* one.

PART II

Two Modes of Contradiction in the "Soledades"

En dos edades vivimos
los proprios y los ajenos;
. . .
a mis soledades voy,
de mis soledades vengo.

Lope de Vega

4

Epic and Pastoral

What is displayed on the tragi-comic stage is a sort of marriage of the myths of heroic and pastoral, a thing felt as fundamental to both and necessary to the health of society.

William Empson
Some Versions of the Pastoral

Juan de Jáuregui in his *Antídoto contra la pestilente poesía de las "Soledades"* of 1614 often has a way of throwing into relief by the very violence of his invectives certain features of the poem which might otherwise pass unnoticed.[1] His litany of Góngora's sins against the accepted canons of genre and decorum is one such case. According to Jáuregui, Góngora's principal error in the *Soledades* was to have attempted a work which rivaled the proportions of epic when his muses were more those of burlesque and erotic poetry:

> Digno es Vm. de gran culpa, pues aviendo experimentado tantos años quán bien celebraban las burlas, se quiso passar a otra facultad tanto más difícil i tan contraria a su naturaleza. . . . Deviera Vm̀., según esto, ponderar las muchas dificultades de lo heroico, la constancia que se requiere en continuar un estilo igual i magnífico, tenplando la grabedad y alteza con la dulzura y suabidad intelegible, i apoyando la elocución a ilustres sentencias i nobles i al firme tronco de la buena fábula o cuento, que es alma de la Poesía.[2]

The charge of inability to sustain the heroic mode was aimed directly at the central thesis of the early defenders of the *Soledades* who ascribed both the difficulty and the novelty of Góngora's manner to the conditions for *sublimity* in poetic decorum. Technically orthodox literary preceptism permitted epic or quasi-epic compositions estrangements of ordinary usage, syntax, and images in order to allow the poem's style to reflect the complexity and elevation of its subject. We have seen that Góngora himself claimed in the "Carta" in defense of his inventions on syntax the requirements of a "lenguaje heroico." Jáuregui must admit in principle the validity of the claim, especially in the matter of "voces peregrinas" or neologisms.[3] But he replies by noting that Góngora's pretension to present the pilgrimage of his mysterious hero as a heroic fiction, demanding a corresponding mode of expression, is everywhere disfigured by a "desigualdad perruna." Extracting from the celebrated passage which describes the pilgrim drying his clothes after the shipwreck (I, 34-41) the single verse "y al sol lo extiende luego," he observes laconically, "Lo mismo dixera una labandera."[4] Elsewhere he offers a catalogue of what he calls "domésticos modos" in the *Soledades* and sets this against a list of Góngora's favored *cultismos*; thus "lino casero," for example, comes to oppose "náutica industria," "vomitado"/"triplicado," "bachillera"/"polulante," and so forth.[5]

The satire of the neologisms activates the more serious charge of disproportion. If the heroic indeed admits "arrobamientos," these must in turn correspond to the character of the subject of imitation, canonically epic or tragic. But the themes and scenes of the *Soledades* are to all appearances bucolic, in Jáuregui's words, "concurso de pastores, bodas, epithalamios, fuegos."[6] So Góngora's experiment, where it does not disintegrate because of an inability to sustain heroic decorum, fails because, at best, it works towards an idealization of "cosas humildes." This sense of a disjunction of form and content and affective dissonance was to become the major premise of the anti-*Soledades* school in Spanish literary criticism. Cascales noted succinctly of Góngora's new manner: "Ella no es buena para poema heroico, ni lírico, ni trágico, ni cómico; luego es inútil."[7] The formalist revision of the *Soledades* has, ironically, tended *to agree* in essence with Jáuregui and the *detractores*, simply inverting the terms of judgement and celebrating Góngora's artificiality and the hedonistic pleasures of a poetry liberated from didactic canons. Hence Dámaso Alonso's point about a "puro placer de formas" and Collard's that the *Soledades* represented in the seventeenth century a new literary genre "en que la 'utilidad' desaparece frente al arte descriptivo."[8]

But there is an interesting divergence in the two major replies elicited from Góngora's defenders by the *Antídoto*, the Abad de Rute's *Examen del "Antídoto"* and Pedro Díaz de Rivas' *Discursos apologéticos*, which suggests that this sort of revision may not be completely to the point. The Abad, musing leisurely on "varios pareceres" which might define the type of poem represented by the *Soledades*, concludes that the poem conflates the traditional form of the lyric ode with a "fábula no simple, sino varia y mezclada *a modo de Romance* [italics mine]."[9] He continues:

> . . . supuesto que no es drammático, tampoco puede ser épico, ni la fábula o acción es de Héroe, o persona ilustre, ni acomodado el verso; menos es Romance, por más que tenga del mixto, porque demás de no aiudarle el verso, ni introduce Príncipes por sujeto del Poema, ni Cortes, ni guerras, ni aventuras. . . . Bucólico no es aunque en él entran Pastores, ni Haliéutico, aunque pescadores, ni Cinegético aunque cazadores; porque ninguno destos es sujeto adequado y trata a todos los referidos

es necesario confesar que es Poema, que los admite y abraza a todos: qual sea este, es sin duda el Mélico.[10]

Lorca derived essentially from this position in his remarks on the *Soledades* in "La imagen poética de Góngora." He argued that Góngora meant to produce "un gran poema lírico para oponerlo a los grandes poemas épicos que se cuentan por docenas." But how was he to rival the scope of an epic poem without introducing at least the pretense of a story which could sustain the reader's focus and interest? "Si le daba a la narración, a la anécdota, toda su importancia, *se le convertía en épico al menor descuido* [italics mine]. Y si no narraba nada, el poema se rompía por mil partes sin unidad ni sentido." Thus the story is only a skeleton meant to support the living flesh of the images, Lorca concluded: "no tiene ninguna importancia."[11]

Díaz de Rivas, on the other hand, maintained that the *Soledades* were in effect *a novel in poetic form*: "aquel género de Poema de que constaría la *Historia ethiópica* de Heliodoro si se reduxera a versos."[12] The remark is elicited by Jáuregui's claim that Góngora had used the heroic to illegitimately embellish his bucolic subject matter. The principal theme of the poem, according to Díaz de Rivas, "*no es tratar de cosas pastoriles* [italics mine. Díaz de Rivas says in a marginal note: "Estas materias son circunstancias accidentales al fin principal de la obra"], sino la peregrinación de un Príncipe, persona grande, su ausencia y afectos dolientos en el destierro, todo lo qual es materia grabe y debe tratarse afectuosamente, con el estilo grabe y magnífico." Tasso is cited to prove that an epic may be composed of "materia amorosa," although the commentator hedges his bet in a footnote: "No quiero yo decir por esto que las *Soledades* son obra épica."[13]

The "circunstancias accidentales" seems clearly wrong unless we take it as it was probably meant: in Aristotle's sense that all elements of a poetic representation are contingent on the story. And the issue of the story of the *Soledades* is not the life of the countryside *per se* but rather the pilgrim's relation to this life and the question of what will become of him. The *Ethiopan History* mentioned by Díaz de Rivas was the model for the Byzantine romances that were popularized in Europe in the late sixteenth century. In Spain there are two important examples of this genre before its sublimation by writers like Cervantes in the *Persiles* and Gracián in the *Criticón*: Alonso Núñez de Reinoso's *Historia de los amores de Clareo y Florisea* (1552) and Jerónimo Contreras' *Selva de aventuras* (1565).[14]

Now it is obvious in one sense that Góngora has before him in constructing the *Soledades* the whole tradition of the Greco-Roman and European pastoral. The Abad speaks of the poem as a "pintura que habla" in which "como en un lienzo de Flandes" Góngora has depicted a vast variety of rural scenes, landscapes, exercises, and types.[15] Noël Salomon thinks of an "idylle champêtre" conceived as "un grand poème capable d'égaler par les dimensions les *Géorgiques* de Virgile."[16] But (to answer Lorca's theory), if Góngora had already in Virgil the model of a long descriptive poem on bucolic themes, why then his recourse to the particular device of the pilgrimage to sustain the lyric tension? Why should he "risk" the contamination of epic? The pilgrim's "Bienaventurado albergue" encomium, the repeated references to the middle-state as a bucolic ideal and to the convention of a *concordia discors*, the health and vigor of his shepherds and peasants, their natural generosity and warmth, the wisdom of their elders, the social and erotic ritual of the wedding–all these define the *Soledad primera* as a pastoral comedy. But this is precisely a genre (and a human possibility) *left behind* as the pilgrim continues past the wedding village into the shoreline locales of the *Soledad segunda*. Why the transition? The pilgrim is young, an exile, very much in love. In the future is the hope of a reconciliation with the *belle dame sans merci* that motivates his wandering and makes him oblivious of danger, "inconsiderado peregrino." We are meant to see the pleasant countryside he passes through as a transitional episode in a larger voyage trajectory of disaster and recovery.[17] So it is presented as a moveable landscape which embraces dissonant and contradictory elements and evolves perpetually into new vistas and sensations–no longer the static and vaguely platonized background of the *locus amoenus* but a realistic landscape, full of change, energy, turbulence. The nature of the pilgrim forces him to move as in the epic convention beyond the temptation to remain in the periphrastic idyl. He is like the young Aeneas who must reject Dido in the name of a destiny he does not yet understand, like the separated lovers of Byzantine romance who must move out of the disorder and "pleasant confusion" of the wilderness towards reunion in an urban apotheosis. The city is the monument of *achieved* history, maturity; the world of nature belongs to childhood and adolescence. The pilgrim's "enemiga amada" is the abstraction of the hope of exile, something that is at once an erotic experience of woman and the suggestion of an ethical and political ideal.

What I am saying is that Jáuregui's charge of inconsistent decorum in the *Soledades* is strictly correct but also that this dissonance is *intended* by Góngora. The pastoral is there to harmonize the furor of the epic quest, the epic to embellish nature and the countryside, to make them seem as something moving towards the same goal as the hero. Neither pastoral nor epic by itself is sufficient, so Góngora creates a fiction, the *Soledades*, which is textured by the friction between and within these modes.[18]

The traditional signs of epic in Renaissance poetry are the trumpet, its recreational analogue, the hunting horn, and the sound of military drums and yells–sounds that call forth to battle, that celebrate victory, that announce the ruler. The pilgrim's sleep in the *albergue*–because it is a pastoral oasis from his disaster–is uninterrupted by "trompa militar . . . o *destemplado* / son de cajas" (I, 171-72). The pastoral opposes these metallic harmonics with the natural sound of a stringed instrument or shepherd's reed flute to actualize the idea of its landscape as a quiet space in the turmoil of life: "son dulce" against "son claro."[19] Góngora, however, is often given in his later poetry to building images which "confuse" the two signs of mode. A poem on the tomb of Garcilaso (Millé 405) yields the expected "el corvo instrumento" but also ". . . la ya sonante / émula de las trompas, ruda avena." The panegyric for the Duke of Lerma is nominally an epic set in *octavas reales* which describes the life of the Court and the empire, but Góngora places it under the inspiration of the muse Euterpe:

> bese el corvo marfil hoy desta mía
> sonante lira tu divina mano;
> émula de las trompas su armonía (Millé 420)

The *Polifemo* dedication specifies a "culta sí, aunque bucólica, Talía." Thalia is a muse associated with comedy and rural themes. (Virgil describes her as the muse of his adolescence in the sixth *Bucolic*: "Prima Syracosio dignata est ludere versu / nostra nec erubuit silvas habitare Thalia," which E. V. Rieu renders as "My earliest muse, Thalia, saw fit to play with light Sicilian verse. She dwelt among the woods, and did not blush for that.") "Culta" in the adversative construction is itself a *cultismo*; Pellicer remarked in his commentaries, "*Culta*, limada, perfeta, de modo que aunque manege acciones rústicas las frases estén colocadas con aseo."[20] The poem is set "al son de la zampoña mía"–which is also the instrument Polyphemus chooses to accompany his lament.

Niebla is pictured riding in front of the walls of his estate at Huelva with a falcon on his wrist. The falcon is "templado" which implies "well-trained" and also "in tune" as in music; by preening his feathers he makes the small bell tied around his neck sound. Niebla's horse champs at its bit–"tascando haga el freno de oro, cano / . . . la ociosa espuma"; a hunting dog whines and stretches against a "cordón de seda." These details suggest a "son de caza" which is being held in check, inhibited, in order to allow the transition to the reharmonization of the pastoral: "Y al cuerno, al fin, la cítara suceda." Góngora commands "treguas al *ejercicio* sean robusto, / ocio atento, silencio dulce." "Treguas" means respite or, more precisely, "cease-fire." This will be the time of the poem, the "en cuanto escuchas" he asks of Niebla. The end of the dedication summarizes the movement from the epic furor of the hunt to the subtler labor of reading itself:

> Alterna con las musas hoy el gusto,
> que si la mía puede ofrecer tanto
> clarín–*y de la Fama no segundo*–
> tu nombre oirán los términos del mundo.

Claudio Guillén, looking back at the *Egloga primera*, observed that "peace, harmony in love, or the light of understanding and truth, imply, within a dynamic form, their origin in war, discord and darkness." Garcilaso's idyl of erotic and spiritual consolation is history-framed, "but one moment in a long process of conflict and purgation."[21] In the *Polifemo* Acis and Galatea dwell in a *temporary* refuge from a world of natural and social violence; their paradise will be destroyed by the interruption of Polyphemus' jealous rage. Góngora's sense that his poem will rival the "clarín" in declaring the value of his patron signifies that he means to raise his pastoral "tregua" to a level where it can involve the forces and events which are proper to epic. Pastoral is posed against epic but also becomes epic in its range and power of expression.[22]

The hunting scene of the *Polifemo* is echoed in the last section of the *Soledad segunda*. The subject is again (but now tacitly) Niebla, leaving his castle on the shore with a group of hawkers and their birds, horses, and dogs. Where the *Polifemo* dedication "suspends" the hunt, here Góngora is concerned with unleashing a spectacle marked by a degree of violence previously absent in the body of the *Soledades*. A trumpet is heard over the water calling the procession together: "ronca los salteó trompa sonante" (710). Its harmonics are picked up by the noise of the iron gate of the castle–"el duro son"–and the figures based on metal of the hawking itself, for example, "que en sonoro metal lo va siguiendo" (852).

The *Soledades* begin like the *Polifemo* in an inhibition of the violence and movement of a hunt. The spiraling sentence of the *Dedicatoria* pictures a scene of furious distension: the Duke of Béjar chasing game in the snow-covered mountains–"gigantes de cristal"–of his estates

> donde el cuerno, del eco repetido,
> fieras te expone, que–al teñido suelo,
> muertas, *pidiendo términos disformes*–
> espumoso coral le dan al Tormes (9-12)

This culminates in the articulation of a verbal command–"*arrima* a un fresno el fresno"–which introduces a motion to restrain the violence, to bring it within the exceeded limit.[23] The hunting–in the image of a mother bear kissing the shaft of the duke's javelin–reasserts itself, only to give way to the presentation of an aristocratic *locus amoenus*:

> –o lo sagrado supla de la encina
> lo augusto del dosel; o de la fuente
> la alta zanefa, lo majestuoso
> del sitïal a tu deidad debido– (22-25)

Here the duke is to rest while he listens to (i.e., *reads*) the *Soledades*. But the invitation to the space covered by the "pie acertado" of the lines of verse is framed by the action of the vassals who go out into the woods to raise new game; the duke should allow Góngora only "un rato"–the place of art and recreation in a life of action. To replace the previous "cuerno"of the hunting, Góngora introduces his pastoral muse and instrument:

> Honre süave, generoso nudo
> libertad, de fortuna perseguida:
> que, a tu piedad Euterpe agradecida,
> su canoro dará dulce instrumento,
> cuando la Fama no su trompa al viento. (33-37)

Again the hint of a "confusion" between epic and pastoral. The *Soledades* are a time of pastoral *exile*: a "libertad, de fortuna perseguida" which invites the duke's favor, which is itself corroded from within by the pilgrim's desire for the "enemiga amada" and the form that desire takes, the movement of his "pasos perdidos." The pastoral "dulce instrumento" is echoed in the "lagrimosas de amor dulces querellas" ("segundo de Arión dulce instrumento") of the shipwrecked hero. The terminal "cuando la Fama no su trompa al viento" suggests, however, that the transcendence he aspires to is beyond the unity and harmony of the pastoral and must involve the social and historical landscape of epic. It is this landscape, at once agonic and sublime, which is reintroduced at the end of the *Soledades* with the martial "trompa," the elegant marble castle, and the intricate violence of the hawking scenes.

The pilgrim, then, is the matrix of this modal tension between pastoral and epic. Spitzer once remarked "¿Pero no es cosa sabida que Góngora se pone siempre en escena como peregrino abandonado de todo el mundo?"[24] The pilgrim, who is the very epitome of aristocratic *cultismo*, retains nevertheless a certain affinity with the picaresque Lazarillo. (Góngora draws the ironic parallel himself in a sonnet of 1594.)[25] Like the *pícaro*, the pilgrim is the form of a consciousness which makes its way through the world in a condition of perpetual *homelessness*. His journey is defined by an initial loss of family or community, a fall from innocence and plenitude, and his efforts to find a point of reconciliation with the world: "salir a buen puerto," to use Lazarillo's language. His presence combines in the *Soledades* the sublimation or furor of the epic hero who is carried along by a super-personal teleology of necessity and providence and the secular marginalization of what Lukács called "roofless" characters: Quijote, the *pícaro*, the ambitious provincial, the adolescent, the orphan, in a word, the "problematic" hero. The problem in both cases is symmetrical: the discovery or the creation of a homeland, the landscape and community of the soul. But from *Lazarillo* onwards this will become in the novel the peripeteia of a solitary figure who represents only himself. Góngora's pilgrim is at *dis-ease* with his world, at the margin of accepted thought and society–the meditative figure in Dürer's allegory of melancholy, Baudelaire's urban *flâneur* who is both involved and abstracted, distant.

The pilgrim is deliberately *unmarked* as a character in the *Soledades*. He appears "náufrago y desdeñado, sobre ausente." He is identified variously as "el peregrino," "el joven," "mísero extranjero," "el caminante," "mancebo," "el forastero," "el huésped," "extranjero errante," and "inconsiderado peregrino." The reader will never learn who, exactly, he is or what he is running from, except for the elliptical allusions to the "enemiga amada" and the life of the Court. Jáuregui commented sarcastically in the *Antídoto*:

> Vamos luego a la traza de esta fábula o cuento, que no puede ser cosa más sin artificio i sin concierto, porque allí sale un mancebito, la principal figura que Vm. introduce, i no le da nombre. Este fue al mar y vino de el mar, sin que sepáis cómo ni para qué; él no sirve sino de mirón, i no dice cosa buena ni mala, ni despega su boca. . . .[26]

Vilanova, in his study of the sources of the figure of the *peregrino de amor*, sees him as an allegory of the ontological human subject: "precisa [Góngora] recurrir a un personaje simbólico que, como arquetipo de la condición humana, reuna a la vez un sentimiento de desengaño y de nostalgia y un anhelo de fuga del mundo en busca de la soledad."[27] Molho speaks of a "protagoniste mystérieux, spectateur neutre dont l'intériorité échappe, . . . l'oeil et l'intelligence du poète, qui, par mythe interposé, explore l'univers, avance pas à pas dans son oeuvre et en conduit la genèse errante."[28]

The pilgrim is the victim of a desire he cannot satisfy. His thoughts turn constantly from the beauty he observes to images of death, of funereal monuments. Góngora superimposes over him traces of the ill-fated adolescents of Classical myth: Adonis, Icarus, Cadmus, Narcissus, Acteon, Ganymede, Arion, Pyramus. These are his doubles: archetypes of the hero as searcher, rash and "errant" youth. The "enemiga amada" in turn metamorphoses throughout the poem as the absent term of the search:

> no la que, en vulto comenzando humano,
> acaba en mortal fiera,
> esfinge bachillera,
> que hace hoy a Narciso
> ecos solicitar, desdeñar fuentes (I, 112-16)
>
> Digna la juzga esposa
> de un héroe, si no augusto, esclarecido,
> el joven, al instante arrebatado
> a la que, naufragante y desterrado,
> lo condenó a su olvido. (I, 732-36)
>
> Al peregrino por tu causa vemos
> alcázares dejar, donde excedida
> de la sublimidad la vista, apela
> para su hermosura;

en que la arquitectura
a la gëometría se rebela,
jaspes calzada y pórfidos vestida. (II, 665-71)

"Regiones pise ajenas,
o clima propio, planta mía perdida,
tuya será mi vida,
si vida me ha dejado que sea tuya
quien me fuerza a que huya
de su prisión, dejando mis cadenas
rastro en tus ondas más que en tus arenas." (II, 130-36)

en su madre se esconde, donde halla
voz que es trompeta, pluma que es muralla. (II, 964-65)

The hero of epic and the nature of his quest have a metonymic function as representing in a particular individual the ideals and destiny of a social collectivity. But the pilgrim is a sentimental hero, a general form of the psychology of solitude and narcissism whose proper dimension of action is the idyl, the pastoral landscape of the mind. His doubles are also the naive strangers of the nineteenth century: Byron's Childe Harold, Stendhal's Fabrizio. His enigma is his solitude, his inability to incorporate himself into any of the variety of human situations he passes through.

The achievement of epic is a *nostalgia* in the *Soledades*, something that has to be abandoned reluctantly. Its paradigm in Spanish and Portuguese letters of the sixteenth century, the epic of naval and military colonization, is miniaturized in the story the Arcadian *serrano* recounts to the pilgrim in the *Soledad primera* (366-506). This captures something of the temptation of the distant and dangerous—the Odyssean journey—but what is rendered finally is the tragic hubris of the Conquest, its illegitimacy, its power to make men the captives of false and cruel values in their very domination of other men. The story breaks off as the narrator recalls his personal disaster in the enterprise: the loss of his son and his fortune. He is an epic hero withdrawn from the historical world of the epic, "fallen" through his failure and disillusion into pastoral. He appears, like the *cabrero* of the ruins and the old fisherman of the island (like Góngora himself?), metamorphosed into the bucolic type of the wise elder. The pilgrim, on the other hand, is distinguished by his immaturity and absence of prudence. A part of that incompletion is his apparent lack of access to action, the passive condition of his exile which makes him an observer. He is a hero who aspires to the proportions of epic, whose action consists in becoming something other than he is. Instead of beckoning to the model of the "geómetra prudente" of the island, the pilgrim senses his own destiny in archetypes of disaster brought on by an excess of desire. Like Narcissus he is in love with his own image, but this love brings with it the danger of suicide or annihilation:

> "Naufragio ya segundo,
> o filos pongan de homicida hierro
> fin duro a mi destierro;
> tan generosa fe, no fácil onda,
> no poca tierra esconda:
> urna suya el Océano profundo,
> y obeliscos los montes sean del mundo." (II, 158-64)

The pathway of his pilgrimage mediates the world-consuming movement of this desire and the *concordia discors* of the pastoral idyl. He must first *pass through* the pastoral, learn what it has to teach him about himself, about what is possible and what illegitimate. He will learn, among other things, that he is only a part of creation, one element in the dance of matter–an element that doubts and thinks, one man wandering in the solitude of himself through a world which offers the possibility of the free and fraternal community of men and women:

> The *Soledades* show the course of a sort of river of abundant life in which all living things are swept along: in the river some creatures conflict, others die, but the river is always there. . . . Death itself becomes an illusion as in the case of the Phoenix.[29]

But the pilgrim is also an "unnatural" hero; he moves in and out of sympathy with the fertile cornucopia which surrounds him. Nature is something "left behind," something that can only be regained as an artifice. He exists in fragments of perception which yield always to his inner sense of incompletion and restlessness. On the second night he arrives with the old *serrano* on the outskirts of the village where the wedding is to take place. The two men watch above the buildings a display of fireworks (I, 646-58). The pilgrim praises the spectacle; his host condemns it as an artificial dilation of the normal passage from day to night, an act of dangerous vanity because it risks, like Phaeton, bringing disaster on the villagers: "campo amanezca estéril de ceniza / la que anocheció aldea." The judgement is distilled from his own tragic experience of these technologies. He is a hero who has passed through epic, while Phaeton belongs with the archetype of the ambitious, self-destructive young man which defines the pilgrim. And yet this same pilgrim had assumed the pose of a Horatian disillusion with the Court and politics in the encomium he recites to the shepherds. At one moment he appears as the spokesman for rustic simplicity and a "prudent" integration with nature and his fellow men, at the next as a courtier with hints of the revolutionary who sees nature only as a conceit which masquerades the artifice of the "enemiga amada"–or of his own narcissism.[30]

The nature of this ambivalence brings us back to Jáuregui's claim that the *Soledades* were themselves a literary vanity which disintegrated by force of its contradictions. But we have seen that the contention of genre and mode which Góngora establishes is placed *within* the character of the pilgrim; it defines the alternating terms of a sentimental education in which the partial communion with nature—the "tregua" or "return to the source"—is the necessary condition for developing a *new* mode of epic practice. The patriotic epic and the epic hero *per se* are no longer a genuine possibility for Góngora as an artist who writes in the midst of a growing sense of crisis and decadence in Spain and from a personal stance which is antagonistic to the ideology of Christian and national despotism which sustains the imperialist epics of the sixteenth century. There is still a fascination with its possibilities but, at the same time, the necessity of rendering it as a fragment. The traditional value of the pastoral as a fiction outside of the contingencies of history has also become problematic in the *Soledades*. It can no longer distinguish itself absolutely from the tensions of the reality it escapes nor, in what amounts to the same thing, maintain itself as a unified literary mode. Macrí speaks of a "gusto y fasto gongorino para revelar, en fin, su crisis interna de existencia y de naturaleza, a la manera *invertida* con la que Cervantes caracterizó el idealismo y la sublimidad de la acción humana."[31] One sign of the exhaustion of Renaissance epic and pastoral was the increasing recourse to dramatic representation and the novel at the beginning of the seventeenth century. We know that Góngora was drawn twice to experiment with the *comedia*. (Jammes has an excellent study of the results in his *Etudes*.) That he never attempted a novel, however, seems due in part to an anachronism built into his class ethic and aesthetic: the suspicion of prose fiction, excepting the Byzantine novel, as a "vulgar" genre canonized by Valdés in *Diálogo de la lengua* and passed through the Erasmists on into Baroque humanist circles. But it is nevertheless the example of the novel, of its status as a "mixed" genre, which bears most closely on the *Soledades*. For Góngora as for his contemporary Cervantes in the *Quijote*, the exercise of literature has taken the place of a political and military practice which is no longer available to them. (Both are from the petty aristocracy which depended on this practice to achieve position and fortune.) Like Cervantes' hero, the pilgrim represents a strategy of invention, the vehicle for the creation of a *possible* discourse in a moment of history in which all models and canons have suddenly become obsolete and no longer serve to represent the writer's own contingencies and contradictions, much less the shape and meaning of his culture and society. The *Soledades* anthologize the whole range of Classical and Renaissance poetry but at the necessary cost of rendering this synthesis as conflictive, as shot through with unexpected antagonisms and transformations: a "soledad confusa."

5

City and Countryside

And the land he will come to is unknown—as is, once he disembarks, the land from which he comes. He has his truth and his homeland only in that fruitless expanse between two countries that cannot belong to him.

Michel Foucault
Madness and Civilization

In the early forties there was an instructive exchange between Leo Spitzer and J. P. Wickersham Crawford over the question of the landscape setting of the *Soledades*. Góngora had rather pointedly seemed to abstain from any direct identification of the world through which he moves his persona. Like the Renaissance *utopia*, it appears as something at once plausible and mysterious, accidentally gained through a providential disaster. Colin Smith, referring rather to the Sicily of the *Polifemo*, speaks of a "vaguely antique or Mediterranean" landscape, "evoked as a timeless conjunction of all that Góngora wants it to be."[1] Jáuregui, we recall, complained not about mystery but mystification; the Abad and the defenders countered with the requirements of the *in medias res* beginning and promised the puzzled that everything would be made clear in the continuation of the poem they expected.

Crawford, however, was bent on locating the poem not in an imaginary or "vaguely antique" setting, somewhat similar in character to that of the novels of chivalry (hadn't Cervantes exploded that possibility in the first part of the *Quijote*?), but in a real and contemporary Spanish-Andalusian geography. On the basis of textual evidence drawn principally from the piscatory scenes of the *Soledad segunda*—the reference to the wreckage of the American trade fleets in the fisherman's tale, for example—he argued that the poem described faithfully aspects of the Atlantic coast of Spain around the delta of the Guadiana River near the city of Huelva. Recalling further Góngora's friendship with two of the prominent Andalusian families from this area, the Ayamontes and the Medina Sidonia, he ventured that the particulars of scene in the *Soledades* were drawn from locales in and around their coastal estates: the village of Ayamonte, the family seat at Lepe, the Medina Sidonia castle on the shoreline near Huelva, the islands of the Bay of Huelva, and so forth.[2]

Spitzer regarded this hypothesis as a typical aberration of literary positivism. The *Soledades*, he argued, make up an imagistic "alambique" in which any reference to the real is necessarily dissolved. The piscatory elements of the *Soledad segunda* are drawn more from convention and typology than from anything Góngora might have seen during his visits with the Ayamontes. Góngora's world is half fantasy, half nostalgic archeology, directed precisely against the presence of reality:

> Vossler dice con razón que el héroe de las *Soledades* se ha evadido. . . . La musa gongorina puebla la soledad con una infinidad de "Wunschbilder," de imágines creadas por su imaginación. La realidad no entra, pues, en este cosmos sino rechazada, transfigurada, recreada. . . . El escenario de las *Soledades* no es Ayamonte, es el alma solitaria, la soledad del poeta.[3]

Certainly the *Soledades* are an "evasion," an attempt to reform in art a reality which is perceived as alienating and prosaic. But the character of this evasion, as we have seen in dealing with Góngora's handling of genre and decorum, is overdetermined, betrays contradictory impulses. Could the *Soledades* be both "Ayamonte" and "la soledad del poeta," both an experienced, poetically "remembered" world present on the margins of the *arbitristas'* "affligida España" and Spitzer's *Wunschbilder*, the formalist concept of the text as a utopia of signs? The argument for a specifically Andalusian setting is crucially supported by a remark in Pedro Espinosa's *Elogio del retrato del Gran Duque de Medina Sidonia* (1625) which alleges that the equestrian portrait in the *Soledad segunda* (809-22) pictured the young duke, then also Count of Niebla, in front of the walls of the family castle near Huelva.[4] Espinosa was the poet-in-residence, so to speak, of the Medina Sidonia clan and had reason therefore to know of what he was speaking; moreover, the portrait itself emphasizes the Andalusian character of the prince's horse, which is "espumosa del Betis ligereza."

The "Andalusianism" of the *Soledades* perhaps helps to account for its reception by the Generation of '27 poets and critics who were themselves reacting against the "Castilla como corazón" of the Generation of '98. Lorca noted on Góngora's retirement from the Court to Córdoba in 1609, "Todo el polvo de Castilla le llenaba el alma . . . , y cansado de castellanos y de 'color local' leía su Virgilio con una fruición de hombre sediento de elegancia."[5] This is to agree with Spitzer that Góngora rejects a specific *costumbrismo*, but the celebration of Andalusia in the much-anthologized sonnet "A Córdoba" of 1585 leaves no doubt about the poet's regional loyalties. Leaving Madrid for the second and last time in 1623–"de la merced, señores, despedido"–he announces:

huélgome que es templada Andalucía,
ya que vuelvo descalzo al patrio nido.

Andalusia is both a nostalgic *laudatio temporis acti* for Góngora and a source of suffering, a region particularly devastated by the Spanish crisis of the early seventeenth century. (Recall Mateo Alemán's "Líbrete Dios de la enfermedad que baja de Castilla y del hambre que sube de Andalucía" in *Guzmán de Alfarache*, II, 2.)

Robert Jammes provides here the necessary mediation. "Je me suis attaché à montrer, contre les affirmations d'un certain nombre de gongoristes contemporaines," he writes, "la présence de la réalité, et, plus précisément, de la réalité rurale espagnole des premières années du XVIIe siècle, dans les *Solitudes*."[6] This is not to say that the poem is a portrait of the *actual* conditions of Spanish and Andalusian country life, especially in the context of the increasing breakdown of the rural economy. Góngora draws on Andalusian scenes by first sifting, selecting, and idealizing (by allusion, for example) the data they provide. His landscape "est la fruit d'une longue gestation où agissent à la fois souvenirs de voyage et les joies de la création littéraire . . . contemplé à travers un certain état d'âme." What is formed is a bucolic utopia, "une campagne de rêve."[7]

What are these "souvenirs" in the *Soledades*? A number can be identified with some precision from Crawford's article and Jammes's researches.[8] A visit to Cuenca and its surrounding countryside in 1603, which Góngora had used in the ballad "En los pinares de Júcar" (Millé 52), serves in part as the basis for the description of the procession of mountain folk which occupies the middle part of the *Soledad primera*. The *Dedicatoria* explicitly pictures the hunting estates of the Duke of Béjar near Salamanca, notably as a wintry landscape ("bates los montes, que, de nieve armados") in contrast to the springtime or "southern" mood of at least the first canto.[9] The chain which decorated the Ayamonte castle in Lepe (see, for example, Millé 287) likewise figured in the coat of arms of Béjar, their relative through the Zúñiga clan, to which Góngora commends his poem ("que sus errantes pasos ha votado / a la real cadena de tu escudo").[10] The *Soledad segunda* borrows from a group of sonnets and minor poems dating from around 1607 which describe the life and estates of the Ayamontes, often by recourse to the piscatory mode (Millé 57, 126-27, 283-93, 392-94). It is likely that the village of the wedding in the *Soledad primera* evokes the town of Ayamonte. The Medina Sidonia and Ayamontes were closely related through the kinship complex of, again, the Zúñiga clan. Their estates and castle near Huelva and the town of Niebla itself figure directly in the *Polifemo* dedicatory, together with a portrait of the young Count of Niebla ("ahora que de luz tu Niebla doras"). This castle and the young count, now as the future duke, are the subjects of the last section of the *Soledades*, to believe Pedro Espinosa.

These cases argue for a level of signification which would be accessible to only a limited, but crucial, audience. They suppose that Góngora means to "mirror" in the poem the patrimony and personalities of these aristocratic families, following the pastoral device of transposing from the epic to the bucolic. Each of the elders the pilgrim meets are, for example, "knights" who have retired to the life of the countryside: "Bajaba entre sí el joven admirando, / armado a Pan o semicapro a Marte, / en el pastor mentidos . . ." (I, 233-35). The young prince of the equestrian portrait was noted (like Góngora himself) for his self-enforced absence from the Madrid Court. The point is to see more than the hand of a sycophant here. Góngora is not just hiding the identities of men of power behind these typologies; the hiding itself is meant to "confuse" them, to make them recognize themselves in a different social identity and way of life.

The fisherman of the island, for example, looks out over the ocean from a promontory. The ocean is a "teatro de Fortuna," the setting of empire and conquest:

> . . . ese voraz, ese profundo
> campo ya de sepulcros, que, sediento,
> cuanto, en vasos de abeto, Nuevo Mundo
> –tributos digo américos–se bebe
> en túmulos de espuma paga breve. (II, 402-06)

The intention is to superimpose two landscapes in the image. On the one hand, we are made aware of the Horatian theme of the ocean as the graveyard of civilization, the temptation of death ("Océano importuno"); on the other, of the contemporary and particular situation of Spain's own empire–"tributos digo américos"–which is calculated to inform the aristocratic and intellectual circles of the Court. The vision of navigation as disaster here, as in the earlier nautical epic of the *serrano*, is common enough in Spanish poetry of the late Renaissance. Salomon has studied in some detail the growing tendency in the years following the defeat of the Armada and the consequent loss of naval hegemony to equate the classical meditation on the decline of Rome which produces the iconography of prudent retirement in the Silver Age poets and the contingencies of Spain's increasingly precarious overseas empire.[11] In one of the Ayamonte poems of 1606-07 I have referred to above, a sonnet on the decision of the then marquis to refuse a colonial post in Mexico, Góngora writes:

> Volvió al mar Alcïón, volvió a las redes
> de cáñamo, excusando las de hierro;
> con su barquilla redimió el destierro,
> que era desvïo y parecía mercedes. (Millé 286)

The piscatory Alción is of course Ayamonte himself; the point is to praise him for staying at home, "close to shore" as it were: "Redujo el pie engañado a las paredes / de su alquería." The temptation or illusion resisted is that of "redes de hierro" which would have enclosed him in the intrigue and struggle of courts and empires. Like the fisherman (indeed they are the same "transposition") he is a "prudent geometrician" in preferring to remain in "redes de cáñamo"—Andalusia—although he loses epic status by this decision.

Spitzer was undoubtedly correct in seeing the unfolding scenes of the *Soledades* as a verbal landscape which projects the poet's desire for an order of experience which reality cannot provide. But the problem is historical and not ontological. This landscape is also nourished by Góngora's personal and ideological loyalties. His pilgrim is, in one sense, the poet himself in his Cordoban exile: "náufrago y desdeñado, *sobre ausente*." The terms of this retirement are the decadence of the Madrid Court and the crisis of empire, the ravages of unending war and monetary inflation, the decline of the regional prosperity and power of Andalusia, the sense of a usurping *noblesse de robe* dominating the affairs of the country, the persistence of at least elements of a simpler and less catastrophic life, the nostalgia for childhood, the possibility of a new beginning.

Góngora is much given to using the device of *contaminatio* which he inherits from the Mannerists.[12] The case of the Genoese sailor who appears in the *Polifemo* can serve as an example. Towards the end of his song (*Polifemo*, 449-56), the Cyclops refers to the shipwreck of a "ligurina haya" near his cave. In deference to Galatea, he rescues and lodges one of the crew: "Segunda tabla a un Ginovés mi gruta / de su persona fue. . . ." Góngora's detractors, notably Jáuregui, seized on this as an evident anachronism. The world of the Cyclops belonged properly to the time and space of myth; the presence of a sailor from the "roofless" world of European mercantilist rivalries disintegrates the fiction. The defenders were quick to invoke the authority of Aristotle. Pellicer, for example, commented on the passage in his *Lecciones solemnes* "Pero los poetas con la facultad suya pueden alterar los tiempos, mudar los sucesos, y escribir después lo que fué antes, y antes lo que fué después, de que ay en todos sobradísimos elementos."[13]

We can recognize in the *Polifemo* anachronism which superimposes history and myth the "vaguely antique or Mediterranean" character of the *Soledades*. Everything appears as if a reflex of the world of Hesiod or Horace: "el mísero gemido / segundo de Arión dulce instrumento," ". . . la cuchara, / del viejo Alcimedón invención rara," "urna de Acuario, la imitada peña," "hermana de Faetón, verde el cabello," and so forth. But Góngora also alludes constantly to the known world of European imperial geography and history: "del Ganges cisne adusto," "debajo de la zona aun más vecina / al Sol, calmas vencidas y naufragios," "tórrida la Noruega con dos soles, / y blanca la Etiopía con dos manos," "resplandeciente cuello / hace de augusta Coya peruana," "Tú, infestador, en nuestra Europa nuevo," and so forth. (There is one point where he seems to allow the order of myth to enter directly rather than as decoration by analogy. That is when the fisherman tells the pilgrim that he fears the rape of his daughters by a "sátiro de las aguas, petulante / violador del virginal decoro"–II, 455-64. Otherwise, the *Soledades* are as "plausible" as, for example, *Lazarillo*.)

The proliferation of multidimensional historical and mythic references in the poem acts to sublimate the prosaic reality Góngora starts with. This is not so much a case of escaping from reality as of recreating it. Góngora does more than decorate by allusion; he opens up the world of the poem at any given moment to a series of alternate and parallel landscapes and histories:

El bosque dividido en islas pocas,
fragante productor de aquel aroma
–que, traducido mal por el Egipto,
tarde le encomendó el Nilo a sus bocas,
y ellas más tarde a la gulosa Grecia–,
clavo no, espuela sí del apetito
–que cuanto en conocelle tardó Roma
fué templado Catón, casta Lucrecia– (I, 491-98)

. . . seguida
la novia sale de villanas ciento
a la verde florida palizada,
cual nueva fénix en flamantes plumas
matutinos del sol rayos vestida,
de cuanta surca el aire acompañada
monarquía canora;
y, vadeando nubes, las espumas
del rey corona de los otros ríos:
en cuya orilla el viento hereda ahora
pequeños no vacíos
de funerales bárbaros trofeos
que el Egipto erigió a sus Ptolomeos. (I, 945-57)

Cóncavo fresno–a quien gracioso indulto
de su caduco natural permite
que a la encina vivaz robusto imite,
y hueco exceda al alcornoque inculto–
verde era pompa de un vallete oculto,
cuando frondoso alcázar no, de aquella,
que sin corona vuela y sin espada,
susurrante amazona, Dido alada,
de ejército más casto, de más bella
república, ceñida, en vez de muros,
de cortezas: en esta, pues, Cartago
reina la abeja . . . (II, 283-94)

el borní, cuya ala
en los campos tal vez de Melíona

galán siguió valiente, fatigando
tímida liebre, cuando
intempestiva salteó leona
la melionesa gala,
que de trágica escena
mucho teatro hizo poca arena. (II, 764-71)

The landscape of the *Soledades* becomes in cases like these the simultaneous experience of multiple signs of space and history around the contemplative present of the pilgrim. Góngora punches holes in the visual surface of reality and its perspectival context in order to supercharge the signifying elements, to give them a conceptual density which they lack as objects of immediate perception. It is a landscape which has become scripturalized, which is saturated by the self-memory of discourse as history, which seems compelled to render itself in the artificial form of an emblem or cluster of allusions. But this experience of landscape is also the concretion of the situation of the pilgrim, the furor of his exile which makes his pilgrimage through the poem a phantasmagoria, a search for a homeland which will end his exile, reconcile him to history. Lezama Lima suggests:

> En Góngora, es [el paisaje] un asombro suspendido entre una situación anterior y una sorpresa recién arribada. Aparece el escondido peregrino después que el sueño ha caído sobre las serranas y las fiestas. El sueño viene a borrar la persecución e insistencia de la fiesta, preparando con la caída del ardor de lo anterior contemplado la llegada del peregrino, es decir, alguien que no sabe quién es. Temor de que la presencia y desenvoltura del peregrino se amengüen si penetra en el idéntico paisaje.[14]

The language of the pilgrim's "Bienaventurado albergue" encomium has caused us to take the *Soledades* as a sublimation of Antonio de Guevara's slogan "menosprecio de corte, alabanza de aldea"–the humanist and aesthetic critique of urbanism, bureaucracy, and mercantilism, everything Góngora intuits in the phrase "moderno artificio." We expect instead to be shown a landscape which has been endowed, like the wooden cup the goatherders offer to their guest, with a "forma elegante . . . sin culto adorno." But here we come against the contradiction noted by Jáuregui, the dissonance between Góngora's complication of language and image and the rustic simplicity it is supposed to represent and celebrate. More concretely, we become aware of a curious and reiterated ambiguity in the nominal posture of rejection of the city. Góngora's characteristic strategy is to present a discourse as a kind of "nature," a cornucopia or chaos of signs, then to bring it into a logical order as if a raw material transformed by labor and technique: "limado." By the same token, he is given to representing nature, the *soledad* or wilderness, as if it mimicked the architectonic labyrinth of the city:

Centro apacible un círculo espacioso
a más caminos que una estrella rayos,
hacía, bien de pobos, bien de alisos (I, 573-75)

Mezcladas hacen todas
teatro dulce–no de escena muda–
el apacible sitio . . . (I, 623-25)

Estos árboles, pues, ve la mañana
mentir florestas, y emular viales
cuantos muró de líquidos cristales
agricultura urbana. (I, 701-04)

Los árboles que el bosque habían fingido
umbroso coliseo ya formando,
despejan el ejido (I, 958-60)

These are ways of saying, on the one hand, that nature holds in herself the secrets of all efforts at invention and construction. But then nature would be sufficient knowledge for the pilgrim, and we know that it is the city, "en que la arquitectura / a la geometría se rebela," that holds the secret of the "enemiga amada." Apparently evaded in the pilgrim's exile, it reappears within its bucolic negation, the *soledad*, as a social and aesthetic principle: the round point which encloses all the signs of history and empire, the "mapping" of the variety of nature, the poem as a *fabrication*. Lewis Mumford summarizes the sense of the city I have in mind here:

> It was one of the great triumphs of the baroque mind to organize space, make it continuous, reduce it to measure and order, to extend the limits of its magnitude, embracing the extremely distant and the extremely minute; finally to associate space with motion. . . . The consolidation of power in the political capital was accompanied by a loss of power and initiative in the local centers. . . . Law, order, uniformity–all these are special products of the baroque capital; but the law exists to confirm the status and secure the position of the privileged classes, the order is a mechanical order. . . . The external means of enforcing this pattern of life lies in the army; its economic arm is mercantile capitalist policy; and its most typical institutions are the standing army, the bourse, the bureaucracy, and the Court. There is an underlying harmony that pervades all these institutions: between them they create a new form for social life–the baroque city.[15]

The *Soledades* are not, as we have become accustomed to hear, nature poetry. They depend rather on the convention of the *countryside*, that is, something which is mediated between a pure state of nature (genesis) and the epitome of civilization, the city as apotheosis. This is why the landscape of the poem constantly changes, why the idyllic world of the *Soledad primera* seems to wither under the gaze of melancholy (because that is the condition of its continued meaning). The model Góngora is elaborating is not, as in Jones's idea of a Neoplatonic gnosis, the order of nature posed against the corruption of history; nor is it the static harmony of bucolic *mediocritas*, as in Jammes's reading of the poet's Andalusian "aristocratism." Both are certainly present, but they serve as terms of a dynamic model, the poem itself, which invites the city to be more like the countryside, the countryside more like the city. To put this another way, the *Soledades* are an irradiation of the bucolic by an urban (and historical) intelligence. Góngora is like Prospero in *The Tempest* who withdraws from the corruption of the Court to his island study, only to find that the power of his magic demands that corruption.[16]

The reconciliation of this contradiction can only be tragic. It may be found, I suggest, in those ruins which appear so unexpectedly in the mountain wilderness of the *albergue*:

> "Aquéllas que los árboles apenas
> dejan ser torres hoy–dijo el cabrero
> con muestras de dolor extraordinarias–
> las estrellas nocturnas luminarias
> eran de sus almenas,
> cuando el que ves sayal fué limpio acero.
> Yacen ahora, y sus desnudas piedras
> visten piadosas yedras:
> que a rüinas y a estragos
> sabe el tiempo hacer verdes halagos." (I, 212-21)

The ruins coexist with nature as a monument which has lost its epic stature and human significance. They present the destructive force of history, a power of coercion now dead. They stand now as a product of labor and technique and the interests these have been bent to serve reduced to the state of nature–abandonment and wilderness. They are simultaneously the emblem of melancholy, of a fall from the plenitud and confidence of epic, and of pastoral consolation: "sabe el tiempo hacer verdes halagos." In terms of the central motif of "walling" in the *Soledades*, which L. J. Woodward has elegantly analyzed, the ruins centralize the antithesis between the *albergue* of the *Soledad primera*, a dwelling woven into nature itself, and the marble castle of the *Soledad segunda* which has been rendered immune to nature. To the extent that we have seen Góngora anthropomorphizing nature as a builder, the ruins represent inversely human architecture transformed into an aesthetics of the diffuse and accidental.

We are touching here on a problem that I intend to take up in the third part of this study: to what extent does the pressure of history on the form and theme of the *Soledades* also oblige them to become a representation of history itself? For the moment it is enough to remark that they portray at once the nostalgia for an archaic world alienated by the passage of history and the attempt to discover the form of a "new world" which would escape the contingencies of Spain's national crisis. In a sonnet directed against the critics of his poem, Góngora allegorizes it as a singing bird trapped in the cage of envy and conspiracy woven around it at the Court, seeking its freedom:

Restituye a tu mudo horror divino,
amiga Soledad, el pie sagrado,
que captiva lisonja es del poblado
en hierros breves pájaro ladino.

Prudente cónsul, de las selvas dino,
de impedimentos busca desatado
tu claustro verde, en valle profanado
de fiera menos que de peregrino.

¡Cuán dulcemente de la encina vieja
tórtola viuda al mismo bosque incierto
apacibles desvíos aconseja!

Endeche el siempre amado esposo muerto
con voz doliente que tan sorda queja
tiene la soledad como el desierto. (Millé 341)

Like the "Carta" the sonnet may serve us as the poet's own meditation on the terms of his creation. It yields, certainly, Spitzer's sense of the poem as a process of aesthetic evasion, a retreat from reality into a nature imagined as consolation and pure possibility, into the "apacibles desvíos" of art itself. Góngora asks that the *Soledades* be allowed to leave the Court to return to the landscape—"al mismo bosque incierto"—which is both its inspiration and its proper homeland: Andalusia, or rather the poet's landscape of the mind. But "soledad," like the lamentations of the desert prophets, is also a complaint directed against and to the city, a voice which seeks a *reformation*. Like the Virgilian bucolic it is something that must be brought back from exile to inspire, seduce, and instruct authority: "si canimus silvas, silvae sint consulae dignae" / "prudente cónsul de las selvas dino."

To repeat, the *Soledades* are a dilation of a *time of separation*. The city is the necessary "absent" term of the pilgrimage because the poem is a movement from region to nation, from the archaic utopia of the past to the present crisis of empire, from wilderness to the marriage of nature and technique. But the restoration to the city must also involve a transposition of its initial status as an alienating and alienated home for the poet-pilgrim; his return implies the constitution of a redemptive epic, the triumph of a new form of political and moral imagination discovered in and through the "imperfect" exercise of exile.

PART III

The Architecture of Time

Where the symbol as it fades shows the face of Nature in the light of salvation, in allegory it is the facies hippocratica *of history that lies like a frozen landscape before the eyes of the beholder.*

Walter Benjamin

Allegories are the natural mirrors of ideology.

Angus Fletcher

6

History and Poetic Myth

The action of the *Soledades* seems to take place in an idyllic parenthesis created for the reader by the suspension of the violence of the hunt in the *Dedicatoria* and for the pilgirm by the "fortunate fall" of the shipwreck. Within this parenthesis, Góngora adopts from the Classical and Renaissance pastoral the task of posing a reconciliatory landscape against the pressure of a reality—the world of *negotium* or mere contingency—whose inner forces are not understood and which presents itself therefore as an inexorable fate. The "casi un lustro" of the pilgrim's (and Góngora's own) exile marks the necessary retirement of an urban but alienated sensibility to the nostalgic utopia of a cultural childhood:

> Tus umbrales ignora
> la adulación, sirena
> de reales palacios, cuya arena
> besó ya tanto leño:
> trofeos dulces de un canoro sueño. (I, 124-28)

The world that the pilgrim and the reader will come upon is like the Insula Pastoril which shelters Isea, the Sephardic narrator of Alonso Núñez de Reinoso's *Historia de los amores de Clareo y Florisea*—a space which history has not yet "colonized" where refugees from persecution or disaster may live in peace and equality, and therefore a "deleitosa y suave soledad":

> No les quitaba el sueño si los naos cargados de mercadería, veniendo del Cairo ó de Alejandría, se podrían perder, ni si los bancos gruesos y de gran crédito quebrarían, y en una hora perderían todo aquello que en muchos años habían ganado. No temían que los príncipes los arruinassen, ni de todo destruyessen; no les daba pena sufrir aquellos, á quien todos los oficios hacen malos y contrarios a toda virtud; no les daba cuidado el conquistar reinos, adquirir ciudades, vencer batallas, desear señoríos, querer mandar, buscar las Indias, servir al mundo, perder la vida, destruir el alma. . . .[1]

But we have also seen Góngora's pilgrim represented as someone who cannot find a point of reconciliation with the possible realities he experiences and who moves, step by step, to rejoin the current of history he has dropped out of, in spite of the danger it holds of a "fin duro a mi destierro." His escape from the "enemiga amada" recovers at its extreme limits its point of origin and becomes instead the beginning of a return which is never completed. The *Soledades* seek to take us out of the world of lived experience and necessity into the "apacibles desvíos" of desire matched with a power of invention, into the seeming timelessness of a perpetual Golden Age. But the present constantly intrudes into and contaminates this utopia; the passage of historical time reasserts itself within the ambivalent terms of the pilgrim's search. The end of each sentence/experience is a "little death" or prison the pilgrim feels compelled to flee from into fresh sensations. The landscapes of the poem change, grow older, run down (in the *Soledad segunda*). At the end, the pilgrim is exactly where he began: alone, incomplete, lost. By taking him away from the *immediacy* of the historical present–the tragic epic of the Court and the empire–which distorts his capacity for self-knowledge and change, the poem offers him the possibility of an alternative. Whether he (or the reader) understands this is not insisted upon by Góngora. The pilgrim is a "libertad, de fortuna perseguida." He has to constantly reinvent his freedom; like Don Quijote he will discover that by doing this he is composing his own history.

After the appearance of manuscripts of the *Soledad primera* in 1613 and the discussions they provoked, the Abad de Rute, partly to refute Jáuregui's charge that the narrative elements of the poem lacked substance, indicated that Góngora planned to bring out three more cantos in which, according to the convention of the *in medias res* beginning, the causes and outcome of his wandering would be gradually unfolded.[2] Díaz de Rivas subsequently took this to mean that Góngora intended to construct an allegorical *progress* of the hero through four landscape stages: a "soledad de los campos" (the *Soledad primera* with its pastoral and agricultural themes), a "soledad de las riberas" (the piscatory *Soledad segunda*), a "soledad de las selvas" (hence the "selvatic" conventions of León y Mansilla's *Tercera soledad* in the eighteenth century and similar efforts by the Generation of '27), and finally a "soledad del yermo" which would reconcile the pilgrim to his fate and indoctrinate him into ascetic wisdom. Pellicer some years later conflated this idea of four separate cantos with the conventional allegorical representation of the cycle of human life through the passage of the four seasons of the year:

> Su principal intención fué en quatro *Soledades* describir las quatro edades del hombre. En la primera, la Juventud, con amores, prados, juegos, bodas y alegrías. En la segunda, la Adolescencia, con pescas, cetrería, navegaciones. En la tercera, la Virilidad, con monterías, caças, prudencia y oeconomica. En la quarta, la Senectud, y allí Política y Govierno. Sacó a luz las dos primeras solamente.[3]

Pellicer's hypothesis has certain evident points of contact with the text. It motivates, for example, the device of opening the *Soledades* with an invocation of spring—"la estación florida"—and the youthful character of the lovesick pilgrim, who is, we have seen, a "mancebo" or "adolescente." It has, however, an equally evident defect: how can such a representation of the biographical span of life be compassed by an action which in the two extant cantos takes only five days of the hero's life? In the *Soledad segunda*, neither his age nor the apparent seasonal mode can have changed in the form Pellicer suggested. Taking up this problem in his *Epístolas satisfactorias* of 1635, Angulo y Pulgar concluded that while Góngora had probably intended originally to write four cantos, these were not meant to compose a full biography; they were rather "en similitud" only to the four seasons/four ages allegory. Antonio Vilanova has summarized the sense of these speculations as follows:

> Alegoría de la evasión y el desengaño, simbolizada por la peregrinación de un amante desdeñado que encubre el propio poeta, las cuatro *Soledades* representan la creciente soledad y abandono de la vida del hombre. . . . La condición errante del peregrino, que se enfrenta al quietismo amoroso del pastor, simboliza la fugacidad de nuestra vida, que no detiene jamás su camino hacia la suprema soledad de la muerte.[4]

The formalist critics of the *Soledades*, notably Dámaso Alonso, have been on the whole unsympathetic to the four-*soledad* hypothesis of the Baroque commentators. They retain the idea expressed by Lorca that the pilgrim is a mere device for binding together the succession of lyric set-pieces. It is here, in the intricate texture of sound, sign, and syntax, that the real action of the poem unfolds, not in the vaguely sketched story. Moreover, they suspect correctly that the four-*soledad* hypothesis is contaminated by the post-Tridentine taste for didactic allegories. Pellicer in fact described not so much the actual or possible form of the *Soledades* but rather certain allegorical constructions of Calderón and Gracián's scholastic picaresque, the *Criticón*, which follows exactly the suggested conflation of the four ages of human life, the four seasons, and four landscape stages culminating in Rome as the index of Christian asceticism and sublimation in the face of death. The idea of a "soledad del yermo"—the desert hermitage or ascetic community—suggests at least one possible *completion* of the pilgrim's quest. (Another is the pilgrim's own fear of a "naufragio ya segundo" or "filos de homicida hierro.") But Góngora, at the end of the *Soledad segunda*, seems content to leave his destiny open-ended. The working-backwards-as-the-story-moves-forward characteristic of the plot of Byzantine novels, never actually materializes, at least in the form the Abad de Rute and the other Baroque commentators of the poem thought it would. Consequently, they were at a loss to explain why Góngora appeared to have abandoned the project after such a promising start in the first two cantos.

My own view, which I will develop in the pages that follow, is that the *Soledades* are not unfinished and do not require, in order to explain the mystery of the pilgrim, the hypothesis of a third and fourth canto. Nevertheless, the biographical allegory suggested by the Baroque commentators does represent an important insight into the workings of the poem. What they mistook was simply the form in which the elements of such an allegorical structure are actually present in the two extant cantos. Part of the reason for their mistake was their concern with the story of the pilgrim. But it is not the pilgrim's life which is allegorized in the *Soledades*; it is rather the process of history itself which his aimless wanderings carry before the reader.

Humanist poetics had established the legitimacy of what was termed *historia conficta* or "fabulous" history to account for the practice of poets like Ariosto and Tasso in their grand epics. *Historia conficta* permitted the transposition of legends or myths, chivalric inventions (like Roland), "marvels," and whatnot into what purported to be accounts of actual history. The point was to emphasize "truth to pattern" rather than empirical accuracy. That Roland did not actually exist was not important; what he *represented* in terms of the struggle of Europe with Islam was.

The concept derived from Aristotle's canonic distinction in the *Poetics* of poetry (that is, of epic, tragic, or comic poetic *fictions*) and history. Poetry, he argued, gave the form of the necessary or probable to an action, thereby universalizing the particular; history (or rather what Aristotle and the humanists recognized as historical discourse), as a chronological record of events and persons, could only be an aggregation of particulars, incapable of representing the relations of cause and effect which generated its data. The poet, according to Aristotle, describes "not what has actually happened but the kind of thing that *should* happen (have happened)." In poetic narrative what follows must be seen by the observer as the result, "plausible or inevitable," of what has preceded (*metabasis*). Poetry is thus "more philosophical and more highly serious than history."[5]

This sort of argument is implicit, for example, in Pellicer's defense of the anachronism of having a Genoese sailor appear in the *Polifemo*. His introduction into the mythic space of a Golden Age Sicily was motivated by Pellicer, as we have seen, by the need of the poet to express several dimensions of experience simultaneously. According to the concept of *historia conficta*, the terms of the anachronism should in fact be reversed. Góngora's reworking of Ovid is not "about" the Golden Age. (Góngora in any case does not believe in myth.) Rather, the story of Polyphemus and his destruction of the love of Acis and Galatea is a way of intimating the contemporary conflicts of a mercantilist and nationalist Europe poised between peace and war, agrarian feudalism and capitalism, the new and the old: an erotic and pastoral utopia set against the power of a half-blind giant's jealous greed.

The *Soledades* lie roughly a century away from Vico's *Scienza Nuova* and Hegel's lectures on the philosophy of history, intellectual productions in which we recognize (as we do retrospectively in a Thucydides or Ibn Khaldun) the effort to synthesize Aristotle's two modes of narrative discourse. Góngora and his contemporaries live on an edge of time which separates imperial grandeur from crisis and sterile repression: that is, in a country which has become "historicized," where nothing seems to hold firm. In such a situation the conventional forms of historical discourse—the chronicle, the imperialist epic, the sycophantic political biography—have lost their mimetic force, have become more mystifications of history than attempts to render its inner logic. Hence the need for new forms of representation, Baroque historicism.

"In Mannerist theory," observes G. Carlo Argan, "the historical picture was conceived as an ordered figure group within a predisposed framework: the particular was fitted into a universal space, and history became both a hymn of praise and a monument." The school of Venice introduced in opposition to this conception the idea of painting history as a movement which breaks apart its own spatial and temporal coordinates. Rubens and Baroque painting will attempt to synthesize the two manners, presenting reality as if exploded into fragments by a hidden force, but also showing that this force is not the product of nature or fate but the transforming presence of a history "created and determined by the movements and gestures of the figures, by their heroic furor. The aim is to provoke an emotion and prolong it, to make it last while all the facts and aspects of reality (whether they deal with history or not) are passed in review."[6] To put this another way, in Baroque painting the image of history is no longer that of an individual triumph or pathos set against a static social and natural background. All details of the painting are caught up in the drama of the historical "actor"—an effect which involves the perception of a chaos which is abhorrent and seductive at the same time.

This comes close to a definition of the linguistic flux of the *Soledades*, a flux, moreover, which is produced and determined by the pilgrim's restlessness, his shifting psychic or spatial movements. The pastoral landscape is no longer, as in Garcilaso, a conventional and vaguely platonized *locus amoenus* against which the pain of exile or despair is posed, but rather the necessary product of this pain, the secretion of nostalgia and desire. The pilgrim is *a story* passing through a succession of moments of experience, shaping these moments into units of discourse, then leaving them behind as he moves forward into a new set of contingencies. In this process, the *signatura rerum* of nature, the "script" of recorded history, and the movement of language on the page of the text come together and apart in an intricate dance around the pilgrim. He (or Góngora) is Icarus, child of a labyrinth-maker, now attempting his own "vuelo atrevido":

> "Audaz mi pensamiento
> el cenit escaló, plumas vestido,
> cuyo vuelo atrevido
> —si no ha dado su nombre a tus espumas—
> conservarán el desvanecimiento
> los anales diáfanos del viento." (II, 137-43)

In these terms, which are the pilgrim's own in his soliloquy in the *Soledad segunda*, the biographical allegory suggested by Pellicer does no more than standardize a situation which is already present in the drama of the pilgrim within the two extant cantos. We noted earlier the contrast between his sentimental narcissism and the metonymic function of the traditional epic hero, who both "makes" history and represents in his person the origin and apotheosis of a collective (national, tribal, regional, sectarian, and so forth) historical enterprise. The pilgrim is not so much the *agent* of history–even of his own–as its form of self-consciousness, its "scribe." He is placed between the reader and the metamorphoses of reality described in the *Soledades* in order to create a distancing effect which allows us to compose what is going on, to be able to move from the pleasure Góngora's sentences provoke (the "corteza," to use his own term) to understanding ("lo misterioso que encubren").

The movement of the text composes four clearly distinct scenographic stages in the two cantos which correspond loosely to the time structure of the four whole periods of a day:

(1) The quasi Arcadia of the "Bienaventurado albergue" and the mountain scenes during the procession the next day.

(2) The farmlands and the wedding village in what appears to be a valley below these mountains.

(3) The piscatory, shoreline world of the fishermen and the "breve islote" in the first part of the *Soledad segunda*. (The period of a day outlined in Chapter 3.)

(4) The castle on a hill–"que deja de ser monte / por ser culta floresta"–over the sea which is the site of the violent hawking scenes.

In Jammes's and Salomon's view of the *Soledades* as an Andalusian *Georgics*, these stages are simply synchronic descriptive explorations of different portions of the estates of the Andalusian nobility near Huelva. But there is a certain diachronic logic in their order of succession within the poem. They move, for example, from the simple to the complex, from the crowds of happy *labradores* in the *Soledad primera* to the relatively solitary figures of the *Soledad segunda*, from the pure state of nature of the initial storm and shipwreck to the hermetic artifice of the elegant marble castle at the end: from the archaic to the modern. (Moreover, the *Georgics* themselves are not purely synchronic but rather follow the cycle of the agricultural year.)

Pellicer's hypothesis argued for changes of time and place which were simply not plausible within the limited narrative framework of the two extant cantos. I want to argue, however, that the four scenographic stages in the *Soledades* do involve an allegorical design essentially similar to that anticipated in the four-canto model. In any given society there coexist survivals of previous forms of social and economic organization and anticipations of future developments. In the United States, for example, where capitalism and the commodities market have been the dominant forms of economic activity since the Civil War, there also exist instances of communal tribal societies (the surviving Indian communities), quasi-feudal relations (the share-crop system in parts of the rural South), communities of "brethren" like those of the Shakers or the Amish, various and sundry urban and rural communes and cooperative associations, as well as fairly advanced forms of socialized production (such as TVA) and land ownership (the National Parks System). By the same token, the town or city in feudal society constituted a kind of nucleus of an emerging bourgeois culture and, at the same time, a residue of the Classical past. Side by side with the titular premise of the *seigneur* as master of the land and its "souls," there continued to exist in medieval Europe pre-feudal forms such as the *commons*, or land held and worked collectively by a village, pastoral transhumance rights, usufructure rights of peasants and artisans to their tools and households, residues of private or "yeoman" farming, and so forth.

In this sense, a relatively discrete space and time (like the Andalusian estates of Góngora's patrons) may also reveal on close observation different strata of history and culture present "all at once," so to speak. Each of the first three scenographic stages is based on a different form of economic activity–Arcadian pastoralism, fixed agriculture, fishing and simple manufacture; the last (as well as the dedication) on the exercise of hunting which indexes the leisure and power of the aristocracy. Each presents a corresponding social formation: the goatherd's camp, the rural village, the tiny private estate of the island, the feudal castle with its lord and retinue of servants. Taken together, I am suggesting, these scenes constitute a mimesis of a cycle of historical change, beginning in the genetic chaos of the storm and ending in the violent apotheosis of the hawking scenes.

In attempting such an organization of historical time, Góngora is paraphrasing the sequence of Ovid's version of the myth of the Ages of Metal in the first book of the *Metamorphoses*, which in turn derived from Lucretius' cosmology and sociology in the fifth book of *De rerum natura* and Greek agricultural "almanacs" and myths of creation like Hesiod's *Works and Days* and *Theogony*. In Ovid, the vision of history as a cycle parallel to the cycle of the agricultural year is defined by the succession, involving a progressive "abasement" of value, of the Ages of Gold, Silver, Bronze, and Iron, followed by the destruction of civilization in the Flood and the recommencement of the cycle. Let me recall some of Ovid's text here, since its images are transposed, sometimes rather directly, in those of the four scenographic stages Góngora develops in the *Soledades*.[7]

Ovid proposes to write "a poem / That runs from the world's beginnings to our own days." The initial moment is that of Creation: "Before the ocean was, or earth, or heaven, / Nature was all alike, a shapelessness, / Chaos, so-called." Then, "things evolved, and out of blind confusion / Found each its place, bound in eternal order." Fish, beasts, and birds were each assigned their dwelling; and finally Man was born, who "Alone, erect, can raise his face toward Heaven."

The first millenium, the Age of Gold, was the reign of a perpetual springtime: "there were rivers / Of milk, and rivers of honey, and golden nectar / Dripped from the dark-green oak-trees." In those days, everyone cherished justice and right: "bronze tablets held / No legal threatening" ("nec verba minantia fixo / aere legebantur"). War was unknown:

> Men were content at home, and had no towns
> With moats and walls around them; and no trumpets
> Blared out alarums; things like swords and helmets
> Had not been heard of. No one needed soldiers.

People had not begun to till the land,

> And Earth, untroubled,
> Unharried by hoe or plowshare, brought forth all
> That men had need for; and those men were happy.

With the advent of the Silver Age, Jove divided the year into seasons:

> That was the first time when the burnt air glowed
> White-hot, or icicles hung down in winter.
> And men built houses for themselves; the caverns,
> The woodland thickets, and the bark-bound shelters
> No longer served; and the seeds of grain were planted
> In long furrows, and the oxen struggled
> Groaning and laboring under the heavy yoke.

The Ages of Bronze and Iron introduce the technologies of metal, and with them property and war. In the Bronze Age, men were "quick to arm, / Yet not entirely evil." But, in the Iron Age, all evil was loosed:

> modesty and truth
> And righteousness fled earth, and in their place
> Came trickery and slyness, plotting, swindling,
> Violence and the damned desire of having.

It is the age of nautical imperialism. Pines which had stood on high mountainsides were felled and made into keels to travel the unknown seas. The land, once as free as air and sunshine, was divided into private holdings. Men dug into the earth's "vitals" in search of wealth.

They found the guilt of iron,
And gold, more guilty still. And War came forth
That uses both to fight with; bloody hands
Brandished the clashing weapons. Men lived on plunder.

The gods send the Flood to drown this violence and corruption. The waters rise until

land and ocean
Are all alike, and everything is ocean,
And ocean with no shore-line. Some poor fellow
Seizes a hill-top; another, in a dinghy,
Rows where he used to plough, . . .

As the waters recede, new forms of life begin to appear, "as seed / Swells in a mother's womb to shape and substance." Life begins when moisture and heat are joined:

all things
Come from this union. Fire may fight with water,
But heat and moisture generate all things,
Their discord being productive.

This is the genesis we have observed in the opening section of the *Soledad primera*. The Age of Saturn has returned; the cycle begins anew.

Of course, the *Soledades* are not myth. They describe perfectly plausible scenes and activities in the everyday world of a seventeenth-century countryside. The indexes of an Age of Iron lie *outside* this heterocosmos in the allusions to the life of the Court or to the empire. The action covers only a few days. Nevertheless, Ovid's myth of the Ages of Metal acts as an *informing shape* for Góngora's sequence of representation. The *Soledades* transcend any sort of *costumbrismo*, aristocratic or otherwise. The world of the poem possesses, rather, a kind of exemplary character representing an historical array of social and cultural worlds set against the long-range and short-range cycles of natural time (the period of a day, the cycle of the agricultural year, the span of life forms). By the same token, the pilgrim's story takes the form of a parable in which an individual experience of alienation and conflict becomes paradigmatic. If in such a rendering history seems to be a process which is still not subject to human will, at least it becomes intelligible, with its end points and internal dialectic of change clearly visible.

By conflating the iconography of the Ages of Metal and of Pellicer's biographical allegory with the succession of the four scenographic stages around the axis of the pilgrim's movement, we can generate the schematic model of the *Soledades* found in Figure 1.[8]

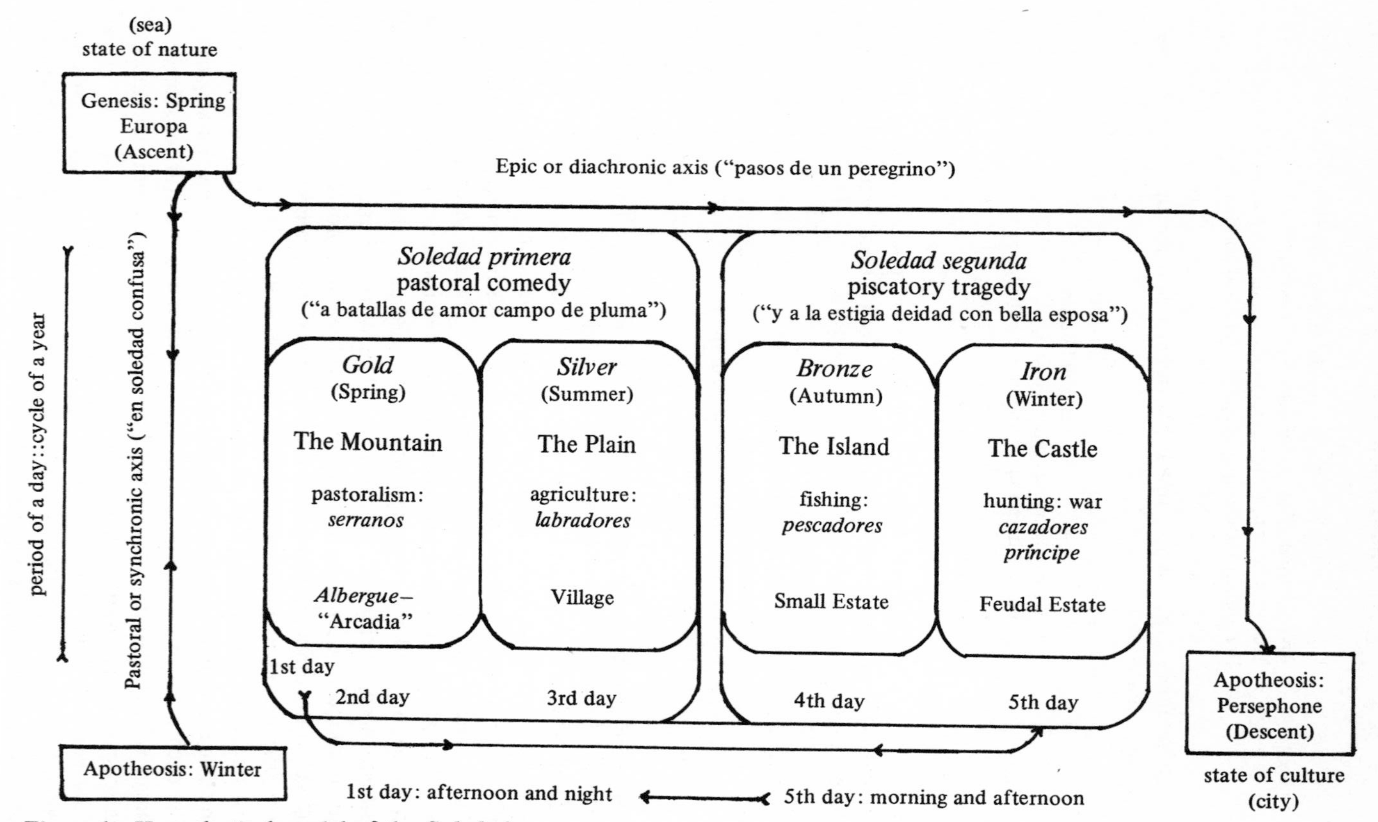

Figure 1: Hypothetical model of the *Soledades*

A number of qualifications are in order before moving on to motivate the various components of this diagram. First, it should be clear that the four seasons/four ages exist in the design of the *Soledades*, to borrow Angulo y Pulgar's reservation about Pellicer's hypothesis, "en similitud" only. Given that the poem begins with the spring equinox, there can be no way in which the final stage, for example, represents an *actual* winter; rather it is more a question of the presence there of signifying elements that function in ways corresponding with the iconography of winter (the idea of death, loss of color, exhaustion, etc.). Although Góngora may indeed have begun with the idea of producing four allegorically distinct cantos (and passed this plan along to friends of his poetry like the Abad de Rute), my reading of the poem argues that he saw the possibility of telescoping what he had hoped to do in these four cantos into a binary pastoral/piscatory, comic/tragic two-canto form. The pilgrim's perceptions of the process he is undergoing are not strictly linear, since they involve instances of remembrance and anticipation. The "disaster" represented by the city is, as we have seen, something he escapes from and desires at the same time. The historicist allusions of the poem are not only to Classical myth but also to such things as the fall of Rome, the dynasties of the Pharoahs and Incas, African and European kingdoms, and the Spanish Conquest. Similarly, there are parentheses in the scenographic stages which are not strictly linear either, in which elements of different "ages" crisscross: the ruins of a castle which suggest that a previous Age of Iron once held sway over the Arcadia of the mountain scenes in the *Soledad primera*, the interpolated epic on the Conquest, the wreckage of the American trade fleets that frames the prudent *mediocritas* of the island community, and so forth. The stages the pilgrim passes through are, after all, *on the edge of* a concrete present which sometimes intrudes into them, just as the storyteller of the first canto and the "viejo Nereo" are figures who have "dropped out" of this reality. The effect is not unlike that achieved in certain utopian novels like Huxley's *Island* or in Carpentier's *Los pasos perdidos*. The fourth stage, the castle, is not, strictly speaking, an "Age of Iron," although I will suggest in my discussion of it that the violence of the hawking scenes is intended as an allegory of war.

The storm and shoreline sequence which begins the *Soledades* has the place of the *cosmologies* of Lucretius and Ovid. It represents Origin: hence the emergence of the pilgrim from the violent dance of the elements much as Virgil's *puer* who brings spring and the rebirth of the Age of Gold. The *albergue* is the antithesis of this genetic chaos: shelter, community, hospitality–the image of nature now bent to human purposes and desires. But it is also a primitive society, barely marked off from nature. (Hence its value in the encomium as a world of innocence in opposition to the corrupting "moderno artificio" which the pilgrim is fleeing.) Like Arcadia the *albergue* belongs in a harsh, but somehow providential in its austerity and simplicity, mountain landscape:

> No pues de aquella sierra—engendradora
> más de fierezas que de cortesía—
> la gente parecía
> que hospedó al forastero
> con pecho igual de aquel candor primero,
> que, en las selvas contento,
> tienda el fresno le dió, el robre alimento. (I, 136-42)

Point by point, Góngora follows Ovid's iconography and its harmonics in the pastoral tradition of the Age of Gold; but the *albergue* also describes a perfectly plausible rural scene in the Andalusian hills. Its inhabitants greet the pilgrim "con pecho *igual* de aquel candor primero." This is to move from myth to history, to something which is *still possible* and which has the character therefore of a *choice*.

The *albergue* is, notably, a society defined economically by pastoralism. It is communal, it lacks fixed agriculture (and hence the construction of dwellings and towns: "retamas sobre robre / tu fábrica son pobre") and manufacture ("limpio sayal en vez de blanco lino"). Compare Ovid's "no trumpets / blared out alarums" with Góngora's

> De trompa militar no, o destemplado
> son de cajas, fué el sueño interrumpido;
> de can sí, embravecido
> contra la seca hoja
> que el viento repeló a alguna coscoja. (I, 171-75)

But the goatherds are also introduced as "worshipping" Vulcan, the god of fire and the forge. Their community exists in harmony with the surrounding nature, but this harmony derives from the marriage of technique and nature, not from nature alone. They are characterized therefore by a "cortesía" which contradicts the "fiereza" of the mountains. Signs of fabrication abound: "limpio sayal," "cuadrado pino," ". . . la cuchara, / del viejo Alcimedón invención rara," "sobre corchos . . . pieles blandas." The epitome of the *albergue* is perhaps the cup of wood from which the pilgrim is invited to drink goat milk: "y en boj, aunque rebelde, a quien el torno / forma elegante dió sin culto adorno."

The continuation of the pilgrim's anabasis on the following day represents a further exploration of the Arcadia sketched summarily in the *albergue* episode, but also a movement in space and time away from the wildness and primitive innocence of this mountain world towards the fertile river valley the pilgrim witnesses with his hosts at dawn. The transition is from the primitive communism of the *albergue* to an agrarian society with its houses and fields, represented by the village in which the wedding is to take place. As in the opening of the *Soledad primera*, this descent is a passage through nature, but a nature which is now domesticated, peopled by moving crowds of hunters and shepherds, boasting ruins, lookouts, pathways which broaden into roads, music, and discourses. The introduction of the wedding party which the pilgrim joins sexualizes the landscape (the *albergue*, like the terminal landscape of the hawking, is a masculine society):

> Vulgo *lascivo erraba*
> –al voto del mancebo,
> *el yugo de ambos sexos sacudido*–
> al tiempo que–de flores impedido
> el que ya serenaba
> la región de su frente rayo nuevo–
> purpúrea terneruela, conducida
> de su madre, no menos enramada,
> entre albogues se ofrece, acompañada
> de *juventud florida*. (I, 281-90)

The tension which had been provoked by the initial allusion to the "mentido robador" and the rape of Europa now reappears shorn of its violence in a play of erotic fragments: "lasciva el movimiento," "inundación hermosa," "montaraz zagala," "el arcaduz bello de una mano," "escuadrón de amazonas, desarmado," ". . . deponiendo amante / en las vestidas rosas su cuidado." These details infect the language of the tragic epic that the old *serrano*, leader of the Arcadian bands, recounts to the pilgrim, as if to associate this drama of discovery, conquest, and loss with the sexual tumescence of the crowd and setting:

> los reinos de la Aurora al fin besaste,
> cuyos purpúreos senos perlas netas,
> cuyas minas secretas
> hoy te guardan su más precioso engaste (I, 457-60)

The epic, like the ruins, is a remembrance of the corruption of a previous Age of Iron that had once held sway over these mountains, a time when "el que ves sayal fué limpio acero." Its heroic cadences are balanced by the songs of the mountain girls which seem to seduce the wilderness:

> Sirenas de los montes su concento,
> a la que menos del sañudo viento
> pudiera antigua planta
> temer rüina o recelar fracaso
> pasos hiciera dar el menor paso
> de su pie o su garganta. (I, 550-55)

As the day progresses, the character of the landscape changes. The initial path through the mountains–"el arco del camino pues torcido" (335)–becomes towards dusk, as other paths feed into it, a sort of bucolic highway: "Centro apacible un círculo espacioso / a más caminos que una estrella rayos" (573-74).

In the distance—"haciéndole atalayas del ocaso"—are the chimneys of the village. At the end of the spiraling anabasis, the pilgrim and the *serranos* will be greeted by a fireworks display above a "templo":

> al pueblo llegan con la luz que el día
> cedió al sacro volcán de errante fuego,
> a la torre, de luces coronada,
> que el templo ilustra, y a los aires vanos
> artificiosamente da exhalada
> luminosas de pólvora saetas,
> purpúreos no cometas. (I, 645-51)

(Góngora's fascination with fireworks is evident in many passages of the *Panegyric* for the Duke of Lerma.) The spectacle, like the dancing which follows, is pleasing but cannot help but recall the austere simplicity of the *albergue* in which "no moderno *artificio* / borró designios, bosquejó modelos."

On the following morning, the pilgrim enters the village itself, which appears as "walled off" from the surrounding fields by its lines of trees and irrigation ditches: Góngora fashions the oxymoron "agricultura urbana" to describe the effect (701-04). The village is part nature, part city—a deurbanized metropolis (like the utopia of the "garden city") or an urbanized *soledad*. The pilgrim, himself a city boy, thus admires "a pesar del estambre y de la seda" the simpler artifice of

> el que tapiz frondoso
> tejió de verdes hojas la arboleda,
> y los que por las calles espaciosas
> fabrican arcos, rosas:
> oblicuos nuevos, pénsiles jardines,
> de tantos como víolas jazmines. (I, 715-21)

Despite its bucolic aspect, this "populoso lugarillo" represents a movement away from the state of absolute innocence. In the Age of Gold "bronze tablets held / No legal threatening" and therefore no marriage or sexual constraint: "vulgo *lascivo* erraba." Here modesty and desire, the civic and the erotic are to be "yoked." The wedding harmonizes the tensions within the world through which the pilgrim has been moving. The procession of the mountain youth—"el yugo de ambos sexos sacudido"—attracted the erotic tumescence and confusion of Pellicer's *adolescencia*. The bridal couple stands instead for the domestication of instinct, adaptation to the economic and social order of a community. They appear after the ceremony

> Del yugo aún no domadas las cervices,
> novillos—breve término surcado—

restituyen así el pendiente arado
al que pajizo albergue los aguarda. (I, 848-51)

Ovid says that, in the Age of Silver, "seeds of grain were planted / In the long furrows, and the oxen struggled / Groaning and laboring under the heavy yoke." The adaptation itself involves a new tension: the necessity of labor, its product as property, the danger that the community will in its very prosperity dissolve into competition, repression, and fratricide. The couple must seek the middle-state, the pastoral *mediocritas*:

Próspera, al fin, mas no espumosa tanto
vuestra fortuna sea,
que alimenten la invidia en nuestra aldea
áspides más que en la región del llanto.
Entre opulencias y necesidades,
medianías vinculen competentes
a vuestros descendientes
–previniendo ambos daños–las edades. (I, 926-33)

The games of the guests follow, as if by reflex of this tension, to portray the discipline and rivalry inherent in the society of the *aldea* turned away from the fury and destruction of war. Hence the concluding epitaph which unites, under the secret presence of Venus, the orders of the martial and the erotic: "bien previno la hija de la espuma / a batallas de amor campo de pluma."[9]

The piscatory *Soledad segunda* restores the pilgrim to the initial seascape, now transformed, however, into a world of fishing and hawking, of boats plying the shores, of groups working and traveling. In Ovid's cycle, the fall of the mountain pine into water–navigation and therefore international commerce–marks the descent into the ages of the lesser metals. The *serrano*'s tragic epic in the *Soledad primera* anticipates the outcome of these new technologies. For the moment, as Jones pointed out, these are still "close to land" activities which conform to prudential norm.[10] But as we move into the world of the *Soledad segunda*, the utopia of the first seems more and more distant. The island miniaturizes the state of *mediocritas*. But what is lost in this limitation is the sense of communal fraternity and celebration which informs the earlier societies. It is precisely a *private* Arcadia in which the social unit has become the nuclear family of the (apparently widowed) old fisherman and his children; the theme is less the ability to collaborate with nature, more the need to transform it, to shape tools and nets, to construct bowers, gardens, shelters, hives, to hunt fish with metal weapons. The table on which the pilgrim is offered his dinner of fishes–"raros todos y no comprados"–materializes the cork on which he slept in the *albergue* as "del árbol que ofreció a la edad primera / duro alimento, pero sueño blando" (II, 341-42. Cf. "Sobre corchos después, más regalado / sueño le solicitan pieles blandas."–I, 163-64.) Where the *albergue* had offered "limpio sayal, en vez de blanco lino," here

> Nieve hilada, y por sus manos bellas
> caseramente a telas reducida
> manteles blancos fueron. (II, 343-45)

We are meant to perceive by these coded transpositions that the island is a society which has developed out of the primitive innocence and simplicity of an Arcadia which is situated just on the edge of the catastrophes of "moderno artificio." Trade fleets passing to and from America litter the shores of the island with "trágicas ruinas de alto robre" (384). The "viejo Nereo," like the earlier *serrano* who had been a protagonist of the Conquest, has retired prudently from this current of history. But his daughters, in contrast, venture out beyond the island to hunt fish in bloodstained waters, each "sorda a mis voces." The hunting is a liberation from their domestic chores, but it involves also an excess–an inversion of "proper" sexual roles–and a danger. Jammes observes among the "dissonances" which he feels mar the *Soledad segunda* a "tendance au romanesque" in these scenes, noting the use of proper names which are nowhere evident in the *Soledad primera.*[11] But these are there to signify that the unitary collectivity of the wedding has been lost. The individual and not the group has become, for good or bad, the protagonist. The mood is set by the piscatory "queja" or love-complaint. The spontaneous fraternity of the *albergue* and the kinship relations which bind together the society of the village are partially in doubt. The pilgrim, because he carries within himself a division between self and other, past and future, desire and reality, now must become an actor in the poem, must intervene, for example, to have the father, at the end of this section, accept the two lovesick fishermen as sons-in-law (II, 635-44).[12]

The norm of the middle-state is maintained only with difficulty in the world of the island. With the pilgrim's departure past ". . . azotadas rocas / que mal las ondas lavan / del livor aún purpúreo de las focas" (II, 686-88), the landscape loses even this coherence and gives way to a climactic violence and disproportion. The marble castle which appears on the shore cliff represents, as we have previously noted, the opposite term of the initial *albergue*–a construction placed over and against nature, the "moderno artificio" excluded in the encomium. The metallic dissonance of the hunting horn sets the appropriate mode. The social praxis, which before had been "close to nature" in communal or patriarchal forms, metmorphoses into hieratic action. The figure who appears at the end of the hawking procession as the climactic typology of the poem manifests the singular authority of a ruler: "la alta mano / de cetro digna." (Compare the retired navigator of the *Soledad primera* who tells the pilgrim that the Arcadians have *appointed* him their leader–I, 516.) His command is signified, in the manner of the equestrian portrait of the prince, by the control he exercises over his Andalusian stallion.

The hawking scenes which follow counterpoint, by their parallel location and their virtuosic character, the games in celebration of the wedding. Those, despite the Pindaric figurations of the athletes' abilities, were exercises on the "heavy" element of earth; the hawking invites the lightness and freedom of the air, attracting by analogy the tragic or potentially tragic spectacles of navigation described in the miniature epic and the fisherman's tale. The dog who casually greeted the pilgrim in the *albergue* reappears as a purebred hound; the horses, hawks, and hunters of the procession seem like an army on the eve of battle, purposively inhibited and set into order:

> tropa inquïeta contra el aire armada,
> lisonja, si confusa, regulada
> su orden, de la vista, y del oído
> su agradable rüido. (II, 716-19)

If before, the principle of harmony and grace had seemed to be the ability to collaborate with nature, the theme of these scenes is rather that of the capacity to master and exploit nature, to pervert nature against herself. The hawks are trained to hunt and kill not in the service of domestic utility but to provide an amusement for the prince, a spectacle which is, however, like the artifice of the poem itself, "agradable" (II, 719, 937). The different hawks, each carefully described, anthologize the political geography of Europe and its colonial empires: "la generosa cetrería, / desde la Mauritania a la Noruega" (737-38), "el girifalte . . . honor robusto de Gelanda" (753-54), "el baharí, a quien fué en España cuna / del Pirineo la ceniza verde" (758-59), "el borní, cuya ala / en los campos tal vez de Melíona [Africa] / galán siguió valiente" (764-66), "el azor britano, / tardo, mas generoso" (786-87). Their aerial battles are "confused" with the terms of military and naval tactics: "Rápido al español alado mira / peinar el aire por cardar el vuelo" (863-64), "Auxilïar taladra el aire luego / un duro sacre, en globos no de fuego, / en oblicuos sí engaños" (910-12), "al viento esgrimirán cuchillo vago" (840).

One senses close to the surface of these acrobatics the poet's intention to portray the larger epic drama of the European wars which are so much the dominant context of his perception of the present. Beyond the hawking scenes, Góngora pictures an abandoned village along the shoreline:

> Ruda en esto política, agregados
> tan mal ofrece como construídos
> bucólicos albergues, si no flacas
> piscatorias barracas,
> que pacen campos, que penetran senos,
> de las ondas no menos

aquéllos perdonados
que de la tierra éstos admitidos. (II, 946-53)

The image of the rude *albergue* had always carried before in the poem the idea of the union of civility and nature. But the village here suggests instead desolation and uncertainty. The inhabitants have vanished; only a brood of chickens remains, protected by the mother hen—"voz que es trompeta, pluma que es muralla" (965)—against the depredations of the fighting hawks who swoop down on them. One is tempted to take this as an epitaphic image of the Spanish and European towns and fields ruined by war, economic collapse, depopulation—a premonition that beyond the pastoral "tregua" of the *Soledades* lies the labyrinth of the Thirty Years' War and the continued disintegration of a Spain divided against itself. Ovid:

Piety lay vanquished,
And the maiden Justice, last of all immortals,
Fled from the bloody earth.

. . .

The end of the cycle in the *Soledad segunda* is *not yet* the landscape of Court and empire: that will be the pilgrim's tragic homeland on "the next day." But it is a simulacrum of this landscape. The experience of history as usurpation and disaster (but also *possibility*) models the form of the *Soledades*. As Salomon has shown, the achievement of political legitimacy in the *comedia* necessarily involves the immersion in the bucolic, which will serve to indoctrinate the prince in the principles of prudence and virtue. To govern well, he must know his people's own capacity for freedom, the nature and extent of their suffering, the "other" possibilities of life and community which still exist in the countryside. The geometric and social labyrinth of the city hides this from him; he must leave it, leave his identity and his class, become "one of them." We have seen that in Góngora the pastoral Age of Gold is no longer a landscape *outside* of history, a dream of an impossible wholeness and grace. It becomes instead a landscape tableau to be read on the panels of the Court where its redemptive value as a social and moral prescription will have to be deciphered. "Soledad" or "edad de Sol." (Góngora on the image of America in the elegy for Medina Sidonia: ". . . Aquella / ara del *Sol edades* ciento.") The Flood, which comes to abolish the disorder of the present and prepare the return of the Golden Age, is the poem itself: something which "confuses" the normal terms of experience, throws us back to our beginnings, atomizes, and reforms.[13]

This is not the place to detail the intricate turns of Góngora's political ambitions, which seem to oscillate between opportunism and disillusion, the favor of the Court and exile. Jammes's *Etudes* serve well enough for that. What should be kept in mind is something we have touched on before: Góngora acts directly or indirectly in his poetry as a representative of and, in the sense of poet-*vates*, a poetic "legislator" for a certain party of the Andalusian nobility and the dynastic, economic, intellectual, and political interests it stands for. He does this because he sees in the power of these families the satisfaction of his own ambitions. He is himself only nominally a part of this aristocracy; more decisively he belongs to that shifting and imperiled "middle" between the great landowners and their retinue in the state apparatus and the peasants, artisans, workers, and beggars of Lazarillo's Spain. Góngora is a contradictory figure, both in his values and in his perceptions. But he is sycophantic only when it serves his own vision of things. This is not, as Robert Jammes is sometimes wont to suggest, a seeking for esteem that contradicts his true feelings, but rather a strategy, like the *Soledades* themselves, to seduce the intellect of the masters of society, to make the person addressed–the "enemiga amada"–more like the poet and the poem; or, as Góngora asks of the Duke of Béjar:

templa en sus ondas tu fatiga ardiente.

We know that in Góngora's day there is a struggle for supremacy at the Court between rival power groups induced by the general crisis affecting Spanish society. Lezama Lima asks the necessary question about the stakes of this game: "¿Por qué los dos mejores amigos de Góngora tuvieron muerte misteriosa, pasados a cuchillo?"[14] The answer is difficult to separate out of the web of political and personal intrigue which surrounds the ministry of the Duke of Lerma. In basic form, however, the struggle involves the opposition of a pacifist party, favoring a critique of mercantilism and its damaging effects on the domestic economy (and thus tied at least nominally to Lerma and the Spanish-Dutch Peace of 1609) and an imperialist party wishing to continue Spain's monopoly of precious metals and its military hegemony over Europe and the Mediterranean. Góngora belongs with *arbitristas* like González de Cellorigo (1600), Pedro de Valencia (1605), and Fernández de Navarrete (1616) in the radical wing of the first; his nemesis Quevedo belongs in the second. The outcome is all but decided by the fall of Lerma in 1618 and the subsequent rise of Olivares. For Góngora, this is the condition of his second fall from grace at the Court and his eventual retirement to Córdoba, where he dies in 1627.[15]

Thirteen years later, in consort with the Portuguese and Catalan uprisings of 1640, the Medina Sidonia captain a rebellion to break Andalusia away from the domination of Madrid and the Hapsburgs. The effort fails, but the political and social forces it involves lend, in retrospect, a certain note of prophecy to the equestrian portrait of the young Duke of Medina Sidonia in the *Soledad segunda* (809-23): ". . . por lo que siente / de esclarecido y aun de *soberano*."[16]

"La obra es un pasatiempo: viejas anécdotas, muecas clásicas. Es tambien un 'pastiche,' que sobrepasa a sus altos modelos en cada tema de las artes de evasión. No 'pinta' el mundo, sino que, mejor que un tratado erudito, desmonta sus mecanismos," writes Pierre Vilar of the *Quijote*.[17] The *Soledades* are neither a civic utopia in the manner of More or Campanella nor, as in the *arbitristas* or the Physiocrats, an ingenious secular model of economic parity designed to mediate relations between the capitalist and feudal sectors and between both of these and the absolutist monarchy. They do share with such constructions, however, a nostalgia for human *equilibrium* combined with the knowledge that the achievement of such an equilibrium cannot be based solely on the restoration of feudalism in its archaic form (the reactionary utopia of Quevedo's "Epístola satírica y censoria") nor, for that matter, on the Arcadian idealism of the pastoral. The partisan ambition of the *Soledades* is to be a subjective "mirror of princes" in the form of a prelude to a new sense of value and social harmony. The dilation of the parenthesis of pastoral exile represents the creation of a time of discourse necessary for the reformation of consciousness in which the spectacle of history can be reviewed at leisure and evaluated. As L. J. Woodward has noted, the end of the poem will pose a choice: the communal landscape of health and providence of the wedding village or the landscape of war and exhaustion, of the "fatal acero," of the hawking scenes.[18] Góngora cannot decide, perhaps because he senses that the solution is bound up with both possibilities.

7

The End of Time

Caso que fuera error, me holgara de haber dado principio a algo; pues es mayor gloria en empezar una acción que consumarla.

Góngora
"Carta en respuesta"

Lucien Goldmann speaks of Racine's *Phèdre* as "the tragedy of the hope that man can live in the world without concessions, hopes or compromises, and the tragedy of the recognition that this hope is doomed to disillusion."[1] This definition comes close to the terms of the paradox we have seen Góngora wrestling with in the *Soledades*. The allegorical scheme of the Baroque commentators was meant to project a completion of the journey interrupted by the shipwreck. But the pilgrim fits strictly only the period of adolescence in Pellicer's hypothesis; he is a form of *incompletion* of character: "el mancebo." The *Soledad primera* begins in the stormy chaos of early spring and moves with its crowds of shepherds and peasants into the summertime world of the wedding. It portrays a tumescent landscape, culminating in the love-making of the bridal couple. The *Soledad segunda*, by contrast, is increasingly austere in mood. Góngora's palette of color is tempered; the final scenes are rendered essentially in black and white—the tones of winter, of writing itself.[2]

This leaves us with a problem. The two cantos, I have tried to show, compose at least tacitly a complete cycle of representation; they are not "unfinished" as we have come to believe. But, as every reader of the poem will have discovered, the ending of the *Soledad segunda* comes rather abruptly. We expect the pilgrim, as before, to come upon a new shelter and new hosts as the evening of this fifth and final day approaches, perhaps in the castle on the shoreline. But the poem simply stops, leaving him "cosido a la playa" in a rowboat, his origins and his destiny as much an enigma as ever. Jammes has noted the fact that the *Soledad segunda* is some hundred verses shorter than the first, suggesting that Góngora probably intended two cantos of approximately the same length but gave up on the second before reaching this goal.[3]

We have seen, however, that Jammes and many other critics of the *Soledades* do not take the *Soledad segunda* seriously in any case. For them, it is a pastiche of poetic fragments lacking the unity of theme and construction of the first, so the question of this apparently indeterminate ending does not seem a pressing one. But it is clear that the *Soledad segunda*, far from being a casual afterthought, represented for Góngora a *necessary* development. The *Soledad primera* stands by itself as a poetic form presenting the image of a pastoral utopia; but, like the first part of the *Quijote*, it is something that comes to be a *nostalgia* as we continue with the pilgrim into the adventures of the second canto. The wedding is the *concordia discors* of a psychic and social pastoral which begins in the image of Europa and the bull. But the pilgrim participates only as a spectator, a "forastero." The beauty of the peasant bride evokes in him the memory of his own beloved, the "enemiga amada" whom he both flees and desires:

> Digna la juzga esposa
> de un héroe, si no augusto, esclarecido,
> el joven, al instante arrebatado
> a la que, naufragante y desterrado,
> lo condenó a su olvido. (I, 732-36)

But it also establishes her *absence* and his inability to find in the community of the *Soledad primera* the image of his own self-completion. He is an aristocrat who is also "inconsiderado." He remains at the end of the *Soledad primera* still the exile—"náufrago y desdeñado, sobre ausente"—whose quest must continue forward in a landscape driven beyond pastoral consolation.

Góngora lacked neither the time nor the creative energy to provide at least a nominal ending for the *Soledad segunda*. The difficult burlesque *romance* on the theme of Pyramus and Thisbe, for example, appears to have been written soon after the *Soledad segunda*. Moreover, we know that Góngora reworked the last sections of the *Soledad segunda* several times. On the urging of friends, he was to add a forty-three line coda (937-79 of the present text of the *Soledad segunda*) for Chacón's projected edition of the *Soledades* around 1622.[4] His critics, however, were fond of noting his apparent inability to sustain and complete his poetic projects. Faria y Sousa spoke of a "falta de fuerças, para concluir las obras le atava è impedia: sino diganme sus devotos, porque no acabò la obra, que empeçasse de las que aspiravan à tener cuerpo de principio, medio, y fin?"[5] Góngora's biographers suggest that the second eclipse of his courtly ambitions attendant on the collapse of Lerma's ministry in 1618 may have convinced the poet that there was nothing to be gained by continuing the difficult labor of the *Soledades*.[6] Certainly the web of slander which was spun around the *Soledad primera* in 1613-14 must have also been a factor in modifying Góngora's plan to continue the poem. To have at least "rounded off" the *Soledad segunda*, however, was certainly not beyond his resources. So if the ending appears abrupt and inconclusive, as if the poet had abandoned the poem in disgust or despair, we are forced to conclude that Góngora *intended* this effect.

The suspended ending, which makes the text appear as a "ruin" of the expected form, is not something peculiar to the *Soledades*. Rather, it seems a characteristic strategy throughout his literary production. The case of the long *Panegírico* for the Duke of Lerma is especially interesting in this respect, since it was probably written around the same time as the *Soledad segunda* (that is, between 1613 and 1617). The poem is an attempt to portray the career of Philip's chief bureaucrat using the form of the Renaissance epic. The resulting tension between subject and genre is highly unstable. (Imagine an epic in the style of Pope on Henry Kissinger's travels.) In fact, Góngora really is aiming at a new genre, the sycophantic political biography in verse. But his portrait of the *privado* is curiously selective. The pastoral muse Euterpe is to preside over the poem rather than the expected "trumpet" of epic. Lerma is presented not as a warrior but rather as a prudent diplomat and administrator, a man of conversation and festivity. The biography breaks off suddenly, as if Góngora had lost interest in continuing it because of Lerma's sudden disgrace in 1618. The final section describes his negotiation of the Spanish-Dutch peace treaty of 1609. The last *octava* allegorizes the deposition of arms:

> A la quietud de este rebelde polo
> asintió el Duque entonces indulgente,
> que por desenlazarle un rato solo,
> no ya depone Marte el yelmo ardiente
> su arco Cintia, su venablo Apolo,
> arrimado tal vez, tal vez pendiente
> a un tronco éste, aquélla a un ramo fía
> ejercitados el siguiente día.

Recall the "arrima el fresno a un fresno" of the dedication to the Duke of Béjar which inhibits the spiraling violence of the hunting scene. This last *octava* seems a rather calculated way to abandon the biography. Jammes notes: "sous la plume de Góngora, le duc de Lerma devient une sorte de 'prince de la Paix.' Image idyllique, certes, mais d'autant plus révélatrice: elle n'exprime pas une réalité, mais l'idéal de Góngora."[7]

The incompletion of the *Panegyric*, then, is a product of the pressure of historical contingency on Góngora's exercise of poetic form. A continuation is not possible because it would involve the necessity to depict the intervention of antagonistic circumstances and forces which do not correspond to the poet's ideal. Góngora's experience of history is discontinuous and precarious. This explains his fondness for the epico-lyrical ballad, since it represents a sentimental *episode* broken away from the teleological design of a larger narrative pattern.

The beautiful *Angélica y Medoro*, for example, is an erotic dilation of a brief interruption in the ongoing process of sectarian war depicted in Ariosto's epic. Hence the recourse to the enigmatic or "subjunctive" ending of the traditional *romance*: "el cielo os guarde, si puede, / de las locuras del Conde."[8]

Lukács observed that the problem of form in the novel cannot be posed purely because it is always bound up with a solution of the ethical problem the action of the novel has posed. We have seen, in particular, that Góngora's poetry exists face to face with a historical reality which is constantly eroding its premises. What kind of ending is required by the pilgrim who is, like Lazarillo and the lovers of Byzantine romance, a form of *homelessness*? Góngora has to avoid in the *Soledades* the subjectively imposed idyl—the Insula Pastoril—but also the ethical compromise with an unsatisfactory reality, Lazarillo's marriage of convenience or the absolute withdrawal from the world of Christian asceticism, the *soledad del yermo*. He realizes that the question must continue to be posed but that he cannot answer it within the poem, that the solution demands something created on the "outside" by his reader. So he ends the *Soledades* by appearing not to end them, leaving the equation of necessity and possibility indeterminate.

In studying the structural articulation of the *Soledades* in Chapter 3, I argued that Góngora makes of the first and fifth days of his narrative a single whole period of a day. The fifth day begins with the pilgrim's departure at dawn from the island and ends in the retirement of the hawking party along the beach, apparently in the afternoon; the first begins in the afternoon and passes into twilight and the nocturnal shelter of the *albergue*. Together they form a "day" whose terms have been reversed, whose morning comes at the end of the poem and whose evening comes at the beginning. Moreover, the pilgrim is, at the end, in somewhat the same situation as in the shipwreck scene, traveling in a boat along a shoreline in the afternoon.

This tricked identity of end and beginning was to be exploited similarly by other Baroque writers, most notably Gracián in the *Criticón*. Gracián appeared to divide his novel into three books of thirteen chapters (or *crisi* as he calls them) each. But the last book has in fact only twelve. The *Criticón* begins on the island of Saint Helena where Critilo, like Góngora's pilgrim, is washed ashore after being shipwrecked and meets Andrenio; it ends on another island where the heroes arrive at the apotheosis of their adventure. This Isla de la Inmortalidad is the entrance to the *Civitas Dei* where they will be reunited at last with their absent wife/mother, Felisinda (or the principle of divine grace). Gracián's aim was to illustrate the Baroque sense of time as a cycle: the "wheel" of the four seasons conjoined with the biographic and geographic stages of a pilgrimage which is an allegory for a human lifetime. As in the formula of the Byzantine novel, the spatial-temporal movement is from south to north and from spring to winter. (The *Soledades* begin with an allusion to "el enemigo Noto"—a storm wind of the Adriatic—and end with a reference to a pair of hawks as "los raudos torbellinos de Noruega.") We are meant to understand that the place of the missing final chapter of the *Criticón* is taken by the island of the first–Saint Helena or the state of nature. The resulting structural conceit invokes the didactic theme of the cyclical character of human and natural time. The death of the text establishes the emergence of a new cycle of life, a new pilgrimage; Gracián's heroes, however, are liberated from the pattern of recurrence through the labors they perform on their journey and enter the absolute time of a "Mansión de Eternidad." Góngora's conflation of the first and fifth days obeys a similar morphological principle. It defines the *Soledades* as a cyclical spectacle in which end and beginning, past and present, are joined together. (Góngora's favorite emblem is the phoenix.)[9]

Tacit in this sort of construction is the unity of beginning, middle, and end of representation that Góngora's critics found lacking: first day (afternoon and evening: the shipwreck and *albergue*); the three whole periods of a day (the Arcadian procession, the wedding, the island); final day (morning and afternoon: the castle and the hawking scenes). The pattern of the pilgrim's wandering may thus be represented as follows: [embarcation], shipwreck, shoreline, inland anabasis, descent to the river valley, stasis (in the wedding village), reappearance on the shoreline, passage on water (the fishing scenes), pseudo-anabasis (the tour of the island), embarcation, stasis (during the hawking scenes), [disembarcation, in the indefinite future beyond the poem, the "next day"].

The final day of the *Soledades* returns to the genesis landscape of the shipwreck, once wild and confused in the gathering twilight, now radiant in the early morning, crowned by the elegant artifice of a marble castle standing on the shorecliff above the ocean. The pilgrim is traveling along a rocky beach stained with blood from the fishing of the previous day in a small skiff; it is dawn. The castle appears as if in contrast to the "azotadas rocas" in the distance:

> en la cumbre modesta
> de una desigualdad del horizonte,
> que deja de ser monte
> por ser culta floresta,
> antiguo descubrieron blanco muro,
> por sus piedras no menos
> que por su edad majestuosa cano (691-97)

As the skiff approaches, the pilgrim is fascinated by the translucent walls which seem like the body of a woman:

> mármol, al fin, tan por lo pario puro,
> que al peregrino sus ocultos senos
> negar pudiera en vano.
> Cuantas del Océano
> el sol trenzas desata

contaba en los rayados capiteles,
que–espejos, aunque esféricos, fieles–
bruñidos eran óvalos de plata. (698-705)

The vision brings the pilgrim and the two brothers manning the skiff to a halt, inaugurating a contemplative stasis that will continue until they begin to move along the shore to follow the retirement of the hawking party in the Chacón coda:

La admiración que al arte se le debe,
áncora del batel fué, perdonando
poco a lo fuerte, y a lo bello nada
del edificio . . . (706-09)

The castle is the apotheosis of the progressive series of architectonic forms Góngora has been tracing in the *Soledades* which include the initial nest of the eagle (whose place on the "escollo" the building now occupies), the "retamas sobre robre" of the *albergue*, the ruins, the buildings and fields of the wedding village and the island, and the desolate village of the coda which follows. Unlike these constructions, it conveys a feeling of the eternal and the absolute: a monument closed against time, mirroring in its silver capitals the ritual tragedy of the birth and death of the sun. It seems a symbol of the poem itself as an enigmatic object: something at once massively dense and translucent, walled off from the surrounding drama of nature but also opening out onto it, a "corteza" and the kernel it conceals and protects, something masculine suggesting war and government that has been feminized, a finished artifact still ambiguously open, like the fishing nets "fábrica escrupulosa, y aunque incierta / siempre murada, pero siempre abierta."

In the iconography of Byzantine romance the castle/palace represents the completion of pilgrimage–the full humanization of the hero, his capacity for understanding and rule. Casalduero notes:

En el barroco el lugar inculto era siempre el habitáculo del hombre-fiera, mientras que el lugar culto alberga al hombre-rey, al hombre que se impone a sus instintos, al hombre que manda sobre su naturaleza. Monte-Palacio es, pues, la representación de los elementos que forman la unidad humana. Hay que salir del monte o de las islas desiertas y bárbaras para ir a vivir a palacio, el lugar donde tendrá todas las tentaciones. En el palacio del Mundo–la Tierra–sufrirá todos los engaños de la realidad de los sentidos y la realidad de la inteligencia. El hombre acuciado por el ansia de conocimiento llega siempre a descubrir su propia finitud, su temporalidad; la muerte: este es el fruto de la sabiduría, el fruto del árbol de la ciencia.[10]

The castle in the *Soledad segunda* follows the description Góngora gives in his *Egloga piscatoria en la muerte del Duque de Medina Sidonia* (1615) of the coastal fortress near Huelva, which was the family seat of the Medina

Sidonia. In the *Egloga*, as in the *Soledad segunda*, the building is viewed from a fishing skiff near the shore manned by two brothers, Alcidón and Lícidas:

> Perdona al remo, Lícidas, perdona
> al mar, en cuanto besa
> maravillas no bárbaras en esa
> aguja que de nubes se corona;
> el tridente de Tetis, de Belona
> incluye el asta. ¡Oh cuánto
> sella esplendor, desmiente gloria humana,
> esa al margen del agua construída,
> si no índice mudo desta vida,
> pompa aun de piedras vana,
> urna hecho dudosa jaspe tanto,
> de poca tierra, no de poco llanto!
>
> Erré, Alcidón. La cudiciosa mano,
> siguió las ondas, no en la que ejercitan
> piedad o religión. Sobre los remos
> los marinos reflujos aguardemos,
> que su lecho repitan. (Millé 404)

The parallelism with the scene in the *Soledad segunda* is noteworthy: the shoreline setting, the halting of the movement of the skiff, the "culta floresta" (here "maravillas no bárbaras"), the image of the reflection of the sunlight on the water ("Cuántas del Ocëano / el sol trenzas desata / contaba en los rayados capiteles" in the *Soledades*). The solitary and unnamed aristocrat who emerges from the castle is, we have seen, the young Conde de Niebla also pictured in the *Polifemo*. Niebla was the son of the duke elegized in the *Egloga*, and so here (since the *Soledad segunda* dates from around 1617) the *new* Duke of Medina Sidonia. Niebla was known as an accomplished hawker, a talent Góngora appears to celebrate in the climactic aerial battles of the poem. But this activity, like the construction of the *Soledades*, was an exercise of aristocratic exile undertaken by a young man who preferred the "solitudes" of his Andalusian estates to the intrigue of the Madrid Court. The equestrian portrait reveals not only the image of the prince—"en modestia civil real grandeza"—but also, like the pilgrim, the adolescent, the seeker of solitude and melancholy, the incomplete archetype of a future political authority.[11]

Moreover, the hawking itself has an ambiguous character. On the one hand, it is a sign of aristocratic sublimation; on the other, as I have suggested earlier, it introduces into the peaceful and abundant landscapes of the poem images of violence and plunder. The "ronca les salteó trompa sonante" of the hawking party marks the end of the *idyllic* dilation established by the "reposo" from the hunt in the *Dedicatoria*. The hyperbolic struggles of the hawks seem to explode and exhaust the possibilities of destruction latent in the dialectical tensions within the poem; tensions that, up to this point, Góngora has held in check or unleashed in nondestructive sublimations like the games which follow the wedding. Their "batalla de pluma" is a kind of cataclysm of the text itself which invites the poet's characteristic metonomy of feather for pen and the black and white of script:

> y con siniestra voz convoca cuanta
> negra de cuervas suma
> infamó la verdura con su pluma,
> con su número el sol. En sombra tanta
> alas desplegó Ascálafo prolijas (883-87)

In the version of the text Pellicer reproduced in his *Lecciones*, the *Soledad segunda* breaks off with a graphic image of a dying hawk falling like Icarus, with whom Góngora identifies his pilgrim, into the sea:

> Tirano el sacre de lo menos puro
> desta primer región, sañudo espera
> la desplumada ya, la breve esfera,
> que, a un bote corvo del fatal acero,
> dejó al viento, si no restituído,
> heredado en el último graznido. (931-36)

An obscure passage: does it allude to the disaster Góngora himself suffers in 1618 because of Lerma's fall from power in the "golfo de pesadumbres" of the Court? Is it an unconscious or an intentional allegory of the failure of the *Soledades*, of Góngora's ambition to make his poetry a mode of understanding and reconstructing a Spain locked by the interests of its dominant class into a spiral of war and economic prostration, now rendered "desplumada"? L. J. Woodward has noted of it:

> Góngora is asking us to contemplate the utter loneliness of the human soul—"breve esfera del viento"—when it is trapped by its stupidity and avarice, and thereby condemned to a terrified flight between two fixed limits of certain death. Its end is a croaking—"último graznido"—which the wind inherits, like the puncturing of a ball. This squalid death is at the hands of a tyrant into whose power its own greed has placed it.[12]

The *Soledades* seem in the end like a discourse which has emptied itself of of any possibility of fresh poetic life. The necessity of this negation must be seen in the context of Góngora's experience of the economic and political decline of his country and of his own frustrated ambitions in the brief decade between the fall of Lerma's ministry and the poet's death in 1627. We are very distant in these final scenes of the *Soledad segunda* from the joyous and fraternal community of the wedding village, presided over by the goddesses of love and agriculture.

Góngora was to add during these years the coda of forty-three lines to the *Soledad segunda* for the private edition of his poems planned by Juan Chacón. It is a section which simply resonates the images of death and exhaustion in the hawking scenes, a concluding gesture of abandonment and despair. Leaving Madrid for the last time in 1623, he would write to a friend (or to himself), in anticipation of his death, lines like these:

¿qué prudencia del polvo prevenida
la rüina aguardó del edificio?

La piel, no sólo sierpe venenosa,
mas con la piel los años se desnuda,
y el hombre, no. ¡Ciego discurso humano! (Millé 373)

que presurosa corre, que secreta,
a su fin nuestra edad. A quien lo duda,
fiera que sea de razón desnuda,
cada sol repetido es un cometa.

¿Confiésalo Cartago, y tú lo ignoras?
Peligro corres, Licio, si porfías
en seguir sombras y abrazar engaños.

Mal te perdonarán a ti las horas;
las horas que limando están los días,
los días que royendo están los años. (Millé 374)

En la capilla estoy y condenado
a partir sin remedio de esta vida;
siento la causa aun más que la partida,
por hambre expulso como sitiado. (Millé 376)

The Genesis of the *Soledad primera* presented the spectacle of nature placed against the deep infinity of the universe: the hyperluminosity of suns and stars, the violent dance of the four elements, the sexual convulsions spreading outwards from the union of Europa and her "mentido robador"; an atmosphere of radiance but also of turmoil and confusion; the springtime agony of birth; the heaving together of water, wind, and land, storm, shipwreck, and lovesickness; the promise of sensual intoxication–Dámaso Alonso's "halago de los sentidos"–and the enticement of romance; travel in unknown lands, mystery, desire; a seemingly limitless horizon of fresh sensations, of gentle people and gentle places; a beginning. In antithesis, the images of the Chacón coda: a weary hawking party moving along a shoreline stained with blood and the broken bodies of birds; a desolate, empty village; a dissonant screeching; an owl's wing which blots out the sun:

A media rienda en tanto el anhelante
caballo—que ardiente sudor niega
en cuantas le densó nieblas su aliento—
a los indignos de ser muros llega,
céspedes, de las ovas mal atados.
Aunque ociosos, no menos fatigados
quejándose venían sobre el guante
los raudos torbellinos de Noruega.
Con sordo luego estrépito despliega
—injuria de la luz, horror del viento—
sus alas el testigo que en prolija
desconfianza a la sicana diosa
dejó sin dulce hija,
y a la estigia deidad con bella esposa. (966-end)

The owl is Ascalaphus, the betrayer of Persephone. The initial allusion to the rape of Europa marked the coming of spring; the abduction of Persephone by Pluto—"la estigia deidad"—announces the descent of the year into winter, the death of nature. Persephone's mother is Ceres, the goddess of agriculture celebrated in the hymeneal choruses of the *Soledad primera*. She is able to force Pluto to return her daughter; but Pluto establishes the condition that Persephone must not have eaten anything in the Underworld. Innocently, she has sucked the seeds of a pomegranate; Ascalaphus witnesses this and, to gain the favor of his master, betrays her to Pluto. She will be permitted to join her mother for only a part of the year, after which she must return to the darkness and to her marriage with death. Her ascent will be spring, her descent winter. Ceres, enraged, metamorphoses Ascalaphus into an owl—the omen of evil—and devastates the agriculture of Sicily, turning it into a desert.

The *Soledades* are framed by the counterpoint of a myth of ascension and a myth of descension. As an *idyl* they are Europa: enchantment, sensual intoxication, vertigo; as a *history* they must be abandoned like Persephone to despair and disillusion. Dawn and evening, the limits of the period of a day, the rise and fall of empire, the collective euphoria of the *Soledad primera*, the melancholy of the *Soledad segunda*. But the owl is also the sign of vision in darkness, of the world fading to the senses and appearing as a being of reason to the mind. In Hegel's *Aesthetics* it is the "grey on grey" of prose dialectics which will rise, like the owl of Minerva, above the sunset of a poetic radiance which is condemned to extinguish itself at the very moment it reaches the inner and outer limits of its possibility. Mallarmé: "je vais voir l'ombre que tu devins" and the poem as a "shipwreck" of language itself, *Un coup de dés*.[13]

The effect of Góngora's truncation of the *Soledad segunda* is to alienate the reader from the poem, to force him to complete it somewhere else and in another language. The achievement that is left behind is the creation of a momentary vision of the *Hispanic—un rato—*which is not bound up in the protracted historical crisis of a country that has pushed to the end point its contradictions, its inability to come to terms with history. The appeal beyond is to the kind of community Spain might become "another day." Perhaps this is why Latin American writing continues to bear the imprint of Góngora, because it has had to undertake the search for a *possible* culture and society that would transcend its past and present condition of impoverishment and dependence. For Góngora and the Spain of his day, this appeal was barren; the poet retires again into the night of exile and the solitary wisdom of the study, warning only "Peligro corres, Licio, si porfías / en seguir sombras y abrazar engaños." But it is an appeal that must be renewed, for the disappearance of the pilgrim at the end of the *Soledades* simply marks the entrance of the reader onto the stage of the present.

Notes

Introduction

[1] Maurice Molho, *Sémantique et poétique: à propos des "Solitudes" de Góngora* (Bordeaux: Ducros, 1969), p. 13.

[2] "Technology discloses man's mode of dealing with Nature, the processes of production by which he sustains his life, and thereby also lays bare the mode of formation of his social relations and of the mental formations which flow from them"–Karl Marx, *Capital*, I (Moscow: Foreign Languages, 1961), p. 872, n. 3. This may serve to indicate one of the differences that separate my conception of the *Soledades* from R. O. Jones's seminal "Neoplatonism and the *Soledades*," *BHS*, 40 (1963), 1-16, as well as from C. Colin Smith's rebuttal to Jones in "An Approach to Góngora's *Polifemo*," *BHS*, 42 (1965), 217-38. Both argue that the *Soledades* are a "nature poem," Jones seeing a sort of Baroque *Enneads*, Smith arguing instead that Góngora's representation of nature approximates Darwinian evolutionism. I have preferred to follow the lead of Jones's own earlier "The Poetic Unity of the *Soledades* of Góngora," *BHS*, 31 (1954), 189-204, which portrays the poem as a study of the *relation* between nature and technology. On this point see Bruce Wardropper, "The Complexity of the Simple in Góngora's *Soledad primera*," *The Journal of Medieval and Renaissance Studies*, 7 (1977), 35-51.

[3] In "The Poetic Unity," noted above. Elsewhere Jones wrote: "Part of the underlying theme of the poem is the vanity of opposing Nature, which destroys artifice and punishes presumption. . . . The youth joins a party bearing gifts to a marriage feast. The gifts are common birds and beasts, but all described in terms of exotic splendour: coral, gold, mother-of-pearl, sapphires, rubies. The point seems clear: this is the wealth of Nature, better than all the illusory riches of the Indies"–*Poems of Góngora* (Cambridge: The University Press, 1966), p. 26.

[4] Christopher Caudwell, *Illusion and Reality: A Study in the Sources of Poetry* (New York: International, 1967), p. 80.

[5] *Etudes sur l'oeuvre poétique de Don Luis de Góngora* (Bordeaux: Féret et Fils, 1967). Jammes's introduction, especially the section titled "Idéal de Don Luis" (pp. 26-35), gives an excellent summary of Góngora's conflicting loyalties and perceptions as a provincial aristocrat without means and of the general economic dislocation threatening the status of the petty aristocracy in Spain during the reigns of Philip II and Philip III, including the problem of the "inflation of honor" (the acquisition of titles of nobility by the *nouveaux riches*) which contributed to the marginalization of old noble families like Góngora's.

6 *Etudes*, p. 31.

7 Martín González de Cellorigo, *Memorial de la política necesaria y útil restauración de la república de España* (Valladolid, 1600), *2.ª parte*, fol. 25v. In the same essay he writes: ". . . el no haber dinero, oro ni plata, en España, es por averlo, y el no ser rica es por serlo: haziendo dos contradictorias verdaderas en nuestra España, y en un mismo subjecto" (*1.ª parte*, fol. 29r).

8 "Pues si la palabra *crisis* define el paso de una coyuntura ascendente a una coyuntura de hundimiento, no hay duda de que entre 1598 y 1620–entre la 'grandeza' y la 'decadencia'–hay que situar la *crisis* decisiva del poderío español, y, con mayor seguridad todavía, la primera gran crisis de duda de los españoles"–Pierre Vilar, "El tiempo del *Quijote*," in his *Crecimiento y desarrollo: Reflexiones sobre el caso español*, Spanish trans. (Barcelona: Ariel, 1964), pp. 431-32. On the Spanish crisis of the early seventeenth century and its implications for the *Soledades* I have also found useful Vilar's "El problema de la formación del capitalismo" in the same volume; Eric Hobsbawm, "The General Crisis of the European Economy in the Seventeenth Century," *Past and Present*, 5 and 6 (1954), 33-53, 44-65; Jaime Vicens Vives, *Manual de historia económica de España*, 4th ed. (Barcelona: Editorial Vicens-Vives, 1965), pp. 375-479; and, as a survey, Chapters 8 and 9 of J. H. Elliott's *Imperial Spain: 1469-1716* (New York: New American Library, 1966), especially pp. 296-320. Until Jean Vilar's long-promised study of the *arbitristas* appears in print, a useful introduction to the themes of *decadencia* and *declinación* in the political and economic thought of the day is J. H. Elliott's "Self-perception and Decline in Early Seventeenth Century Spain," *Past and Present*, 74 (1977), 41-61. On the disastrous situation of the Spanish countryside (a reality counterposed in the images of an agricultural utopia in the wedding day of the *Soledad primera*), see Noël Salomon, *La campagne de Nouvelle Castille à la fin du XVIe siècle* (Paris: S.E.V.P.E.N., 1964); the same author's *Recherches sur le thème paysan dans la "comedia" au temps de Lope de Vega* (Bordeaux: Féret et Fils, 1967); and the sections on agriculture in Bartolomé Bennassar's brilliant reconstruction, *Valladolid au siècle d'or* (Paris and The Hague: Mouton, 1967). On the depopulation of America as a consequence of the ravages and forced labor imposed by the Conquest and the colonial crisis which developed as a result, see Woodrow Borah, *New Spain's Century of Depression* (Berkeley: University of California Press, 1951), who estimates a population decline of *90%* on the central plateau of Mexico between the years 1519 and 1607.

9 L. J. Woodward, "Two Images in the *Soledades* of Góngora," *MLN*, 76 (1961), 784. *Arbitristas* like Pedro de Valencia or González de Cellorigo, according to Vicens Vives, "son los que, siguiendo las directrices de la escuela cuantitativa de Salamanca . . . , reaccionaron contra el ideal de acumulación de moneda y abogaron por la reconsideración del trabajo productivo como elemento básico de la riqueza" (*Manual*, p. 412). Pierre Vilar cites the following from one of Valencia's essays:

> El daño vino del haber mucha plata y mucho dinero, que es y ha sido siempre . . . el veneno que destruye las Repúblicas y las ciudades. Piénsase que el dinero las mantiene y no es así: las heredades labradas y los ganados y pesquerías son las que dan mantenimiento. Cada uno había de labrar su parte: ahora los que se sustentan con dinero, dado a renta, inútiles y ociosos son, que quedan para comer lo que los otros siembran y trabajan. (*Crecimiento y desarrollo*, p. 204.)

10 *Crecimiento y desarrollo*, p. 441.

Chapter 1: Góngora's "Carta en respuesta"

1 *Cartas filológicas*, I (Madrid: Espasa-Calpe, 1930), p. 220.

2 In *Temas y problemas de la literatura española* (Madrid: Guadarrama, 1959), p. 150.

3 In his *Etudes*, pp. 28-29 and Appendix II: ". . . on peut admettre que Góngora a eu dans ses veines, comme beaucoup d'autres Espagnols des milieux urbains, un peu de 'sang-juif'; mais tout indique . . . que lui-même ne fut jamais amené à se considérer comme descendant de 'conversos.' " On the other hand, "il faut dire aussi que ses origines andalouses ne pouvaient que le rendre très sceptique–comme beaucoup de citadins de son temps–sur le chapitre de la 'limpieza de sangre.' "

4 Andrée Collard, *Nueva poesía: conceptismo, culteranismo en la crítica española* (Madrid: Castalia, 1967), p. 102.

5 Cited from the version in Dámaso Alonso, *Estudios y ensayos gongorinos* (Madrid: Gredos, 1960), p. 87. As is well known, the article had something of the character of a manifesto for the "poesía pura" of the Generation of '27.

6 In the late seventeenth century the Portuguese critic Faría y Sousa maintained that Góngora's poetry lacked what he called a "misterio scientífico." Espinosa Medrano replied that it was not the business of poetry to constitute a science or corpus of natural doctrine. The novelty of the *dispositio*, not of the *materia*, was what should be appreciated in a work like the *Soledades*; Góngora had nothing to do (nor should he) with the Neo-Scholastic poetics of an "arte docente." A. A. Parker notes a similar distinction in Gracián's *Agudeza y arte de ingenio*: "Since the object of *ingenio* is beauty, not scientific truth, its *agudeza de artificio* is distinguished from the *agudeza de perspicacia* which characterizes philosophers and scientists–the clarity of mind that can perceive and analyze relations and differences that are logical and objectively true"–*Polyphemus and Galatea: A Study in the Interpretation of a Baroque Poem* (Austin: University of Texas Press; Edinburgh: University of Edinburgh Press, 1977), p. 38. Espinosa Medrano's *Apologético* was reprinted by Ventura García Calderón in *Revue Hispanique*, 65 (1925), pp. 397-538.

7 Emilio Orozco Díaz has collected a number of his studies on the beginnings of the debate over the *Soledades* in *Lope y Góngora frente a frente* (Madrid: Gredos, 1973). Pages 168-88 deal with the two initial letters, giving slightly different texts than those in Millé. Andrés Mendoza, Góngora's agent in Madrid, also replied to the "Carta de un amigo" in a letter which Orozco Díaz reproduces and which is of great interest. Lope and/or his cohorts counterattacked with a long "Respuesta." Millé (Epistolario 128) has a "Carta echadiza" of around 1613 by another enemy of the *Soledades*, but this is of lesser importance.

8 *Lope y Góngora*, p. 185. The French Baroque poet Saint-Amant noted similarly about his heroic idyl *Moise Sauvé*: "Il y a un sens caché dessous leur écorce qui donnera de quoi *s'exercer* à quelques esprits" (italics mine). But he cautions too that "dans le recherche qu'ils en pourront faire, peut-être me feront-ils dire des choses à quoi je ne pensai jamais"–cited in Gérard Genette, "D'un récit baroque," *Figures II* (Paris: Seuil, 1969), p. 200.

9 For the text of Serrano de Paz's proposition see "El Doctor Manuel Serrano de Paz, desconocido comentador de las *Soledades*," in Alonso, *Estudios*, pp. 518-30.

[10] R. O. Jones, "Neoplatonism and the *Soledades*," p. 15. See also C. Colin Smith's critique of Jones in "An Approach to Góngora's *Polifemo*" and Jones's rejoinder "Góngora and Neoplatonism Again," *BHS*, 43 (1966), 117-20.

[11] As cited by Noam Chomsky, *Language and Mind* (New York: Harcourt, Brace & World, 1968), p. 8, who adds: "The reference here is to true creativity and exercise of the creative imagination in ways that go beyond normal intelligence and may . . . involve a 'mixture of madness.' "

[12] The claims of both Tasso and Góngora may derive from the same source, Zuccari's concept of a *disegno interior* (a modern rendering might be "inner form" or Gestalt) in the artwork. As Erwin Panofsky detailed, Zuccari and the Mannerists wanted to shift the notion of mimesis away from a representation of the mere phenomenal appearance of an object or action. The *disegno interior* in effect platonized Aristotle. What Aristotle termed the *dianoia* or idea in mimesis was in his *Poetics* simply a contingent aspect of the *mythos* or plot-form, not the organizing principle of the work itself. Zuccari argued instead for an art which represents the generative mental intuition or *anamnesis* of the artist in composing the work and of the viewer or reader in decoding it. See Panofsky's *Idea: A Concept in Art Theory* (Columbia: University of South Carolina Press, 1968). In this sense, for example, the "action" of the *Soledades* is on one level that of poetic intelligence itself, as Góngora suggests in the equation of "pasos" and "versos" in his proposition (see n. 24 below). A. A. Parker adds: "Góngora's *culteranismo* was not a bolt-from-the-blue in 1613 but the cultivation of a steadily developing aesthetic. . . . Beginning with Fernando de Herrera's Commentary (1580) on the poems of Garcilaso, this development constitutes a Platonic poetic stressing the 'divine madness' of the poetic imagination against the Aristotelian discipline of rules" (*Polyphemus and Galatea*, p. 10). On Góngora's relation to Mannerist theory and the Spanish theoretical debates on aesthetics of his time see, for example, Antonio Vilanova, "Preceptistas españoles de los siglos XVI y XVII," in *Historia general de las literaturas hispánicas*, ed. Guillermo Díaz-Plaja, III (Madrid: Editorial Barna, 1953), 281-580; Cedomil Goig, "Góngora y la retórica manierista de la dificultad docta," *Atenea*, 142 (1961), 168-78; C. Colin Smith, "On the Use of Spanish Theoretical Works in the Debate on Gongorism," *BHS*, 39 (1962), 165-76; and Helmut Hatzfeld, "El manierismo de Góngora en la *Soledad primera*," in his *Estudios sobre el barroco* (Madrid: Gredos, 1964), pp. 264-71.

[13] "Góngora seems to be claiming that the mind, puzzling over the multitudinous images, allusions, and tropes of the *Soledades*, is led to an understanding of the source of all truth, which, in terms of seventeenth-century orthodoxy, one might suppose to be God. And yet God is nowhere mentioned in the poem; and even here, in the letter, Góngora seems to be studiously avoiding a name in favor of a philosophical abstraction" (Jones, "Neoplatonism," p. 2).

[14] Gracián himself suggested as much when, after praising Góngora in the Sea of Ink episode towards the end of the *Criticón*, he noted that his "plectro" lacked a string, that of "moral enseñanza." On the relation of Góngora's poetic practice to Gracián's later theory of the conceit, see in particular Parker's careful study in *Polyphemus and Galatea*, pp. 30-50.

[15] *Libro de la erudición poética*, facsimile ed. (Madrid: C.S.I.C., 1946), pp. 11-12. Parker (*Polyphemus and Galatea*, pp. 10-11) mentions a *Cisne de Apolo* by Luis Alfonso de Carballo (1602) as a precedent for the *Libro*.

[16] *Libro*, p. 25.

[17] Millé, Epistolario 2. Américo Castro took the reference to "animales de cerda" as an irony mocking Lope and his cohorts in the "Carta de un amigo" as dolts and would-be *cristianos viejos* or "pork-eaters"–*Hacia Cervantes* (Madrid: Taurus, 1967), p. 23.

[18] In "La *Soledad primera* de Góngora: notas críticas y explicativas a la nueva edición de Dámaso Alonso," *RFH*, 2 (1940), 159.

[19] "La *Soledad primera*," pp. 159-60, n. 1.

[20] In "The Poetic Unity," p. 193. Jones's intention throughout this article is to study the "parallel between the physical and moral order" that Góngora, he thinks, is drawing in the *Soledades*.

[21] "The Poetic Unity," p. 193.

[22] "La *Soledad primera*," pp. 154.

[23] "La *Soledad primera*," pp. 155-56.

[24] Molho, *Sémantique et poétique*. Spitzer noted ("La *Soledad primera*," p. 151): "Hago mía la sugestión de Hermann Brunn . . . de que 'en soledad confusa' se refiere en común a 'perdidos unos y otros inspirados' y que *confusa* significa 'salvaje' (dicho de la maleza) en cuanto se relaciona con *perdidos unos* (pasos) y 'confusa, oscura' en cuanto se relaciona con *otros inspirados*."

[25] Noam Chomsky identifies the main tenet of what he calls Cartesian linguistics as "the observation that human language, in its normal use, is free from the control of independently identifiable external stimuli or internal states. . . . The language provides finite means but infinite possibilities of expression constrained only by rules of concept formation and sentence formation. . . . The finitely specifiable form of each language . . . provides an 'organic unity' interrelating its basic elements and underlying each of its individual manifestations which are potentially infinite in number"–*Cartesian Linguistics* (New York: Harper, 1966), p. 29. On areas of Renaissance linguistics which touch on Góngora's concerns in his letter, see also Michel Foucault, *Les mots et les choses: une archéologie des sciences humaines* (Paris: Gallimard, 1966), especially Chapters 2 and 3; Claude-Gilbert Dubois, *Mythe et langage au seizième siècle* (Bordeaux: Ducros, 1970); and Oreste Macrí's sketch of Herrera's "preocupación científica" in *Fernando de Herrera* (Madrid: Gredos, 1959), pp. 99-117.

[26] Rudolf Geske argues that the interpolated nautical epic should be read, in essence, as an allegory of the process of writing itself–*Góngoras Warnrede im Zeichen der Hekate* (Berlin: Colloquium Verlag, 1964).

[27] See the two versions of his letter to Góngora (1613) in Millé (Epistolario 126 and 126 *bis*) and Dámaso Alonso on the matter in *Estudios*, pp. 297-310. I reproduce here the "primitive" text of the ecphrasis on the river as reconstructed by Alonso, "La primitiva versión de las *Soledades*," in his Góngora, *Obras mayores, I: Las Soledades* (Madrid: Ediciones del Arbol, 1935), 370-71.

28 On Benjamin's sense of Baroque art as Trauerspiel, see Fred Jameson, "Walter Benjamin; or, Nostalgia," in his *Marxism and Form* (Princeton: Princeton University Press, 1971), pp. 68-73. An English translation of Benjamin's thesis on German Baroque tragedy has recently appeared: Walter Benjamin, *The Origin of German Tragic Drama* (London: New Left Books, 1974).

Chapter 2: *Soledad primera*, Lines 1-61: The Pilgrim

[An earlier draft of this chapter appeared under the same title in *MLN*, 88 (1973), 233-48. (Copyright 1973 by The Johns Hopkins University Press.) My thanks to The Johns Hopkins University Press for permission to include it here and to Elias Rivers for his suggestions on improving it.]

1 Although, as I will detail in Chapter 3, Góngora's intention was to present each canto of the *Soledades* as a single, organic *silva* with no stanzaic pauses.

2 Góngora's use of Classical myth is meant to bring to mind not only the figures of myth as archetypes of human qualities but also the stories and relationships they involve. This kind of allusive shorthand allows the reader to construct around the barely suggested narrative presence of the pilgrim a series of psychic and situational analogies in myth which define him as a young and "errant" hero, like Cadmus, Narcissus, Orpheus, Icarus, or Phaeton. In the section we are dealing with here, Góngora must have had before him Ovid's account of the Creation in the *Metamorphoses*, Virgil's celebration of the return of the Golden Age in the fourth *Bucolic* (with its "nascenti puero"), and, perhaps, Socrates' Story of Er in Plato's *Republic* and the topic in philosophical romance of the "shipwrecked soul." See Pamela Waley, "Some Uses of Classical Mythology in the *Soledades* of Góngora," *BHS*, 36 (1959), 193-209.

3 In the *Metamorphoses* and Roman pastoral poetry the image of the tree on the mountainside signifies the reign of Saturn, the Golden Age. The "fall" of the pine into the ocean–as the "leño" of the ship, Góngora's "selvas inconstantes"–marks the violation of nature's proper limits and the consequent decay of society into the conflicts and labors of the ages of the baser metals which will culminate in the imperialist fratricide of the Age of Iron.

4 Note the image of a mother hen protecting her brood from the hunting hawks at the end of the *Soledad segunda*:

> ¡Oh cuántas cometer piraterías
> un cosario intentó y otro volante
> –uno y otro rapaz digo milano–,
> bien que todas en vano,
> contra la infantería, que pïante
> en su madre se esconde, donde halla
> voz que es trompeta, pluma que es muralla! (II, 959-65)

Venus is of course the most brilliant planet of the solar system, so she may be alluded to in this form in the "carro brillante de nocturno día" the pilgrim follows to the *albergue*. Since she is such a central (though often tacit) presence in the *Soledades*, it is worth recalling that in Lucretius's *De rerum natura* Venus signifies the force which guides the "dance of matter" and leads it from the genetic chaos of atomic whirl to the appearance of human society and consciousness. Therefore, she is perhaps an index of Góngora's own materialism or, to borrow Wallace Steven's phrase, of a "poetry of earth."

[5] Compare the pilgrim's account of his own misfortune at the Court in the Horatian encomium which alludes both to the peacock and to Icarus:

> No a la soberbia está aquí la mentira
> dorándole los pies, en cuanto gira
> la esfera de sus plumas
> ni de los rayos baja a las espumas. (I, 129-32)

[6] Michel Foucault, *Madness and Civilization*, trans. Richard Howard (New York: New American Library, 1967), p. 21.

[7] The ultimate appeal is, as R. O. Jones noted, away from the corruption of experienced history to nature. The ego, stepping back from alienation, invokes in the tropes of the *Soledades* the appearance of nature. Nature in turn reflects the operations of language, like the flocks of birds which

> tal vez creciendo, tal menguando lunas
> sus distantes extremos,
> caracteres tal vez forman alados
> en el papel diáfano del cielo
> las plumas de su vuelo. (I, 606-11)

[8] Marx, in an aside on the "precocious childhood" of Greek epic and myth at the end of *A Contribution to the Critique of Political Economy*, ed. Maurice Dobb (Moscow: Progress, 1970), p. 216.

Chapter 3: Structure as Figure in the *Soledades*

[In somewhat different form and under the title "Confusion and Construction in the *Soledades*," this chapter appeared originally in *Dispositio (Revista Hispánica de Semiótica Literaria)*, 3, No. 9 (1978). It appears here with the permission of the editors of that journal.]

[1] On the question of his paragraphing of the *Soledades* (a practice also used by the Baroque commentators of the poem like Pellicer), see Dámaso Alonso's "Notas preliminares" to his Góngora, *Obras mayores, I*, 51-58. It is worth noting here that Alonso also modernized considerably both the orthography and the punctuation of the Baroque texts of the poem, the best of which is generally considered Antonio Chacón's manuscript edition, reproduced by R. Foulché-Delbosc in *Obras poéticas de Don Luis de Góngora*, II (New York: Hispanic Society of America, 1921; reprinted 1970).

[2] In his *Sémantique et poétique*, p. 37, n. 6.

[3] The Vicuña *Obras*, the first printed collection of Góngora's poetry, were published in facsimile by Dámaso Alonso (Madrid: C.S.I.C., 1963). In Vicuña's text of the *Soledades* the only stanzaic marking comes, as in the *Aminta*, in the choruses of the epithalamium of the *Soledad primera*. Chacón's manuscript does have paragraphs but they are considerably longer than Alonso's, which correspond generally to individual sentences. Molho

remarks: "La *Soledad* ne se compose donc pas d'un ensemble de *silvas*, mais d'une *silva* unique de 1091 vers" (*Sémantique et poétique*, p. 37, n. 6).

[4] *Sémantique et poétique*, pp. 36-48. Molho refers to Kurt Vossler's pioneering study on the *silva-soledad* form in Renaissance and Baroque poetry, *La soledad en la poesía española* (Madrid: Revista de Occidente, 1941). Like Góngora's *silva*, Greek nomic verse is a type of astanzaic dithyramb.

[5] In his *Discursos apologéticos* (c. 1615). Text in Eunice J. Gates, *Documentos gongorinos* (México: Colegio de México, 1960).

[6] *Sémantique et poétique*, p. 44.

[7] Cited from Gracián, *Obras completas* (Madrid: Aguilar, 1960), pp. 524-25. Gracián is employing the old *topos* of philosophical romance on the innateness of human intelligence and, therefore, of language. Andrenio's process of observation and discrimination amounts to, in effect, the construction of a language.

[8] For example, in Mozart's *Magic Flute* or in Moratín's *El sí de las niñas*. On the iconography of the period of a day in Renaissance pastoral, see Claudio Guillén's study of figures of time in Garcilaso's poetry in his *Literature as System* (Princeton: Princeton University Press, 1971), pp. 179-87.

[9] To put this another way, Góngora attempts a kind of oxymoronic synthesis of the devices of *amplificatio* and *interruptio* as they are defined in Scholastic rhetoric. His tropes, the *silva* itself, are, like the nets of the fishermen in the *Soledad segunda*, a "fábrica escrupulosa, y aunque incierta / siempre murada, pero siempre abierta" (II, 79-80).

[10] Spitzer observed that Góngora's play on doubling and division "parece en verdad una exteriorización del desdoblamiento del poeta (o del protagonista que observa las cosas como él)" ("La *Soledad primera*," pp. 171-72).

[11] *Figures* (Paris: Seuil, 1966), pp. 37-38.

Chapter 4: Epic and Pastoral

[1] The text of Jáuregui's *Antídoto* is in Eunice J. Gates, *Documentos gongorinos* (México: Colegio de México, 1960).

[2] Gates, pp. 138-39.

[3] Gates, p. 107.

[4] Gates, p. 99.

[5] Gates, pp. 120-21.

[6] Gates, p. 86.

[7] *Cartas filológicas*, I, 218.

[8] Collard, *Nueva poesía*, p. 102. I agree with Collard that the *Soledades* represent a new genre not covered in the canons of previous Renaissance poetics, but not with her additional point about their being purely descriptive in nature. Rather, a *soledad* might be defined as an epico-lyrical narrative in verse dealing with the theme of exile or pilgrimage and set in the wilderness or countryside. It is related to the prose *selva*, derived from imitations of Byzantine romance, which replaces pastoral and chivalric fiction in popular taste by the end of the sixteenth century. Pedro Espinosa was writing *soledades* in this sense before and after Góngora's poem. One could follow the development of the genre by studying the imitative works spawned by the *Soledades*: for example, Polo de Medina's parodic *Ocios de la soledad* (1633), Fonseca Soares's *Soledades* (c. 1650), Soto de Roja's Andalusian *El paraíso* (1652), Salazar y Torres' *Soledad a imitación de Góngora* (1690), Sor Juana's *Primero Sueño*, and León y Mansilla's *Soledad tercera* (1718). See J. Ares Montes, "Del otoño del gongorismo," *RFE*, 44 (1961), 323-49; and Emilio Carilla, "Trayectoria del gongorismo en Hispanoamérica," *Atenea*, 142 (1961), 110-21.

[9] Francisco de Córdoba (Abad de Rute), *Examen del "Antídoto" o apología por las "Soledades."* Text included as Appendix VII in Miguel Artigas, *Don Luis de Góngora* (Madrid: Revista de Archivos, 1925).

[10] Artigas, pp. 424-25.

[11] I am citing the version of Lorca's lecture given in the *Obras completas* (Madrid: Aguilar, 1966), p. 81. Similarly, Dámaso Alonso spoke of a "valor lírico: no épico."

[12] *Discursos apologéticos*. Text in Gates, pp. 51-52.

[13] Gates, p. 52.

[14] María Rosa Lida studied Góngora's adaptation of the Byzantine formula in "El hilo narrativo de las *Soledades*," *Boletín de la Academia Argentina de Letras*, 26 (1961), 349-59. The Erasmists, it is worth noting, had granted the Byzantine novel a certain legitimacy because of its origins in antiquity and its philosophical-moral cast which they withheld from other forms of the novel. Cervantes was finishing up his *Persiles* (published posthumously in 1617), a strict adaptation of the Byzantine formula, at the same time Góngora was working on the *Soledades*. For Góngora, the formula, with its conventions like the shipwreck, the wilderness pilgrimage through a variety of exemplary landscapes, and the figure of the lover alienated from the object of his or her desire, provided the model of a narrative built around the psychology of an aristocratic exile.

[15] Artigas, p. 406.

[16] In his *Recherches sur le thème paysan*, p. 193. Besides the fact that both are agricultural "albums," there is a perhaps intentional structural homology between the *Soledades* and the *Georgics*. Virgil's poem is made up of four cantos, each about 500 lines long. Góngora's has two cantos of about 1,000 lines each, but subdivided into the four major scenographic complexes of the Arcadian mountainside, the wedding village, the island, and the castle.

[17] In Renato Poggioli's view, the Renaissance pastoral is always conceived as an "oasis" or "garden" happened upon in the course of an epic mode of action, that is as a temporary or parenthetical haven but one which can also come to effect the ongoing terms of the

epic enterprise, for example, by making the hero aware of the kingdom of love. See "The Oaten Flute," *Harvard Library Bulletin*, 11 (1957), 147-84, and "The Pastoral of Self," *Daedalus*, 88 (1959), 686-99. Both essays have been republished in Poggioli's posthumous *The Oaten Flute* (Cambridge: Harvard University Press, 1975).

18 Góngora is fond of the Homeric device of inverting pastoral and epic orders: "armado a Pan o semicapro a Marte / en el pastor mentidos" or "a batallas de amor campo de pluma." These are more than merely decorative figures; they intrude on the reader a sense that the world of the poem lies in a precarious balance between war and peace, abundance and disaster, generosity and jealous greed.

19 On the trumpet and related instruments as the sign of epic in Renaissance poetry and Góngora's variations on this *topos*, see Antonio Vilanova's *Las fuentes y los temas del "Polifemo" de Góngora* (Madrid: C.S.I.C., 1957), I, 295-301. See Millé 383 and 385 for characteristic examples of Góngora's cultivation in his early years of the sort of military mini-epic or *canción heroica* popularized by Fernando de Herrera.

20 *Lecciones solemnes*, cited in Vilanova, *Las fuentes*, I, 96.

21 *Literature as System*, pp. 110-17.

22 In Góngora, the pastoral or erotic idyl is always only "un rato." The restoration of epic involves sometimes its sublimation but also sometimes its violent destruction, as in the *Polifemo* or *Angélica y Medoro*.

23 Again, the figure involves a play on the alternation of epic and pastoral: "fresno" as the ashen spear of the hunter/warrior, "fresno" as the tree itself, a component of the shady and peaceful grove where the poet asks the duke to rest awhile.

24 In a note in "Revista de Revistas," *RFH*, 2 (1940), 86.

25 Millé 259. The poet, nursed to health out of a near fatal coma, is Lazarus risen from his tomb. But since he has fallen in love with his nurse and thus entered the service of a "blind master"–Cupid–he becomes also "segundo Lazarillo de Tormes en Castilla." Compare the more melodramatic tone of Millé 258 which refers to the same convalescence:

> Descaminado, enfermo, peregrino
> en tenebrosa noche, con pie incierto
> la confusión pisando del desierto,
> voces en vano dió, pasos sin tino.

26 Gates, pp. 87-88. Thomas Hart, taking the same quotation from Jáuregui as his starting point, has recently given a valuable account of "The Pilgrim's Role in the First *Solitude*," *MLN*, 92 (1977), 213-26. Jáuregui strategically ignores that the pilgrim is meant to appear as an enigmatic and contradictory hero. *Soledad* designates not only the spiritual state of loneliness but also the landscape of exile, the wilderness. Jáuregui, however, ventures an irony on the title which reveals his bad faith: "erró V.M. llamándole inpropriamente *Soledades*, porque soledad es tanto como falta de compañía. . . ."

27 Antonio Vilanova, "El peregrino de amor en las *Soledades* de Góngora," *Estudios dedicados a Menéndez Pidal*, III (Madrid: C.S.I.C., 1952), 421-60.

28 *Sémantique et poétique*, pp. 35-36.

29 Jones, "Neoplatonism," p. 14.

30 Like the Story of Er in the *Republic*, the *Soledades* are the story of a dream, a rendering perhaps of the "parasismal sueño profundo" Góngora speaks of experiencing in his sonnets of 1594. The near death of the pilgrim in the shipwreck suggests that his catastrophe represents the *descent* of consciousness into a world open to multiple overlays of signs or symbolic condensations, as in Freud's idea of a subconscious *Niederschrift*. Taken in this sense, the poem belongs with the tradition of the Baroque phantasmagoria: Quevedo's *Sueños*, the "Cueva de Montesinos" episode in the *Quijote*, Calderón's labyrinths, Sor Juana's *Primero Sueño*, etc.

31 Oreste Macrí, *Fernando de Herrera* (Madrid: Gredos, 1959), p. 26.

Chapter 5: City and Countryside

1 C. Colin Smith, "An Approach to Góngora's *Polifemo*," p. 220.

2 "The Setting of Góngora's *Las Soledades*," *Hispanic Review*, 3 (1939), 347-49. The American trade fleets passed just south of the Guadiana delta and the Ayamonte coastal estates on their way to and from Seville in the seventeenth century. By this reckoning, the pilgrim might plausibly be someone traveling in exile to seek a new fortune in the colonies who is shipwrecked along the Huelva coast. After staying with the *serranos* in the *Soledad primera* (the Huelva region is mountainous in parts), the pilgrim descends towards a river (the Guadiana?) and the prosperous village near it. At the start of the *Soledad segunda* he is back on the seashore. The bay created by the Guadiana embouchure has several islands which could correspond to the piscatory community of the old fisherman and his daughters. Near these islands, on the eastern shore of the embouchure a castle overlooks the Bay of Huelva. This could be the site of the hawking scenes in the second canto. Less plausible, however, is Crawford's interpretation of the wedding in the *Soledad primera* as an allegory of the marriage in 1610 of the Marquis of Ayamonte to his cousin, a daughter of the Duke of Béjar to whom the poem is dedicated.

3 Leo Spitzer, in "Revista de Revistas," *RFH*, 2 (1940), 85. Dámaso Alonso had indicated a preference for an earlier version of the famous sixth line of the *Soledad primera* which read "en dehesas azules pace estrellas" instead of "en campos de zafiro pace estrellas." "Dehesas" suggested to Alonso a "representación inmediata, jugosa, hispánica, andaluza." Spitzer countered that "el mundo de Góngora es un mundo irreal y artificial en que el gusto del terruño, la Heimatkunst, nada tiene que ver" ("La *Soledad primera*," pp. 151-76). But Góngora himself announced in the burlesque tercets which accompany his decision to return to Córdoba and his country estate: "Gastar quiero de hoy más plumas con ojos / y mirar lo que escribo . . ." (Millé 395).

4 Espinosa wrote of the duke: "En esta soledad le halló el príncipe de los poetas, Don Luis de Góngora," and then quotes from the equestrian portrait–*Obras de Pedro Espinosa*, ed. Francisco Rodríguez Marín (Madrid: Real Academia Española, 1909), p. 252. The same figure is also the young aristocrat pictured in the dedication of the *Polifemo* ("si ya los muros no te ven, de Huelva"). He should not be confused with his father from whom he inherits the title of Duke of Medina Sidonia and who Góngora elegized in the *Egloga piscatoria* of around 1615 (Millé 404). The setting of all three portraits, however, is the same.

5 In "La imagen poética de Góngora," *Obras completas*, p. 67.

6 *Etudes*, p. 617.

7 *Etudes*, p. 586. Jammes reminds us "qu'en présentant cet idéal de vie rustique Góngora ne prétend pas évoquer la masse des paysans dans son ensemble, mais seulement les plus riches d'entre eux: il faut bien, de ce point de vue, séparer les chevriers du début (dont le mode de vie rappelle le thème de l'Age d'or, comme le mode de vie du cyclope Polyphème) du jeune marié et du vieux pêcheur, dont les richesses symbolisent l'idéal de l'abondance rustique" (p. 617, n. 87).

8 See especially the section of Jammes's *Etudes* titled "Le paysage et sa genèse," pp. 586-92.

9 That is, a *Castilian* landscape set against the quasi-Mediterranean Andalusian *soledad* of the poem.

10 On the emblem of the chain on the Ayamonte and Béjar coats of arms, see Jammes, *Etudes*, pp. 590-92.

11 In his *Recherches sur le thème paysan*, especially pp. 250-357.

12 An instance that closely parallels Góngora's deliberate anachronism is the unsettling mixture of mythic deities, rendered in the manner of Caravaggio, and the weathered, leering peasants in Velázquez' painting *Los borrachos*.

13 As cited by Jammes, *Etudes*, p. 560, n. 64. Inversely, "la légende mythologique n'est qu'un moyen pour exprimer plus commodément–et parfois plus hardiment–un sentiment personnel, des préoccupations contemporaines" (pp. 561-62).

14 In "Sierpe de Don Luis," *Esferaimagen* (Barcelona: Turquets, 1970), p. 30.

15 Lewis Mumford, *The Culture of the Cities* (New York: Harcourt, 1938), pp. 82, 91. G. Carlo Argan notes: "The taste for the monumental, with its reference to the classical past, suited the ruling classes, who regarded themselves as divinely ordained to exercise power and authority. The 'grand manner' (which is no more than an extension of the notion of the monument to all domains of art) thus became identified with the tastes and culture of the conservative class–which in turn explains why the middle classes began to produce, in rivalry, their own particular form of art"–*The Europe of the Capitals: 1600-1700* (Geneva: Skira, 1964), p. 47. Góngora, who as Jammes has shown is a *déclassé* aristocrat, is addicted to the "grand manner" but uses it dissonantly, as Jáuregui correctly noticed, to describe not the city or the centers of ir[illegible]rial power but rather the countryside. But, as Bruce Wardropper has pointed out, "the natural life consists, paradoxically, of subjecting Nature to the discipline of Art. Cultivation is not, as the myth of the Golden Age would have it, an abuse of Nature's prodigality. . . . The Nature of *Las soledades* is one which has been improved by the rustic crafts of its denizens (including turnery) and is being further improved by sophisticated poetic art. . . . The relation between Art and Nature is not one of being but of becoming" ("The Complexity of the Simple," pp. 48-49). The dualistic tendency to separate urban progress and rural backwardness has been traced by Raymond Williams in his survey of the town versus country theme in English literature, with its ambiguous shifting between images of rural innocence and beauty and urban

disdain for "rural idiocy"–*The Country and the City* (New York: Oxford University Press, 1975), p. 51.

[16] It is worth repeating here that the main defect of Jammes's interpretation of the *Soledades* is his inability to see the logic which carries the pilgrim *beyond* the idealized pastoral commonwealth of the first canto. This movement undoubtedly risks introducing again the perversions of an urban "moderno artificio" that the pilgrim had before evaded, but only because the countryside *per se* is no longer a *sufficient* mode of existence for the pilgrim. It must be "elaborated." The same vacillation is evident, as Jammes shows, in Góngora's own character, which is both nostalgic and ultra-sophisticated. Góngora cannot be the poet of some "lost paradise" of feudalism because such a place no longer exists. The rise of the great cities as corporate monopolies or collective *seigneurs* backed by absolutist centralism and mercantilism in the sixteenth and seventeenth centuries involved, according to John Merrington, "not only a massive shift of human and material resources in favor of urban concentrations, but also a *conquest* over the countryside, which becomes 'ruralised,' since it by no means represented in the past an exclusively agricultural milieu. From being a centre of all kinds of production, an autonomous primary sector that incorporates the whole of social production, the country becomes 'agriculture,' i.e. a separate industry for food and raw materials"–"Town and Country in the Transition to Capitalism," in *The Transition from Feudalism to Capitalism*, ed. Rodney Hilton (London: New Left Books, 1976), p. 171. Marx noted laconically: "the modern age is the urbanization of the countryside, not ruralization of the city as in antiquity"–*Grundrisse*, ed. Martin Nicolaus (New York: Vintage, 1963), p. 479.

Chapter 6: History and Poetic Myth

[Portions of this chapter appeared under the title "The Language of Contradiction: Aspects of Góngora's *Soledades*," *Ideologies and Literature*, 1, No. 5 (1978), 28-56. I am grateful to the Board of Directors of the Institute for the Study of Ideologies and Literature for permission to include them here, and in particular to Nicholas Spadaccini and Edward Baker for their helpful criticisms.]

[1] I am citing the text of the *Historia* (1552) given in B.A.E. III, *Novelistas anteriores a Cervantes* (Madrid: Atlas, 1963), 467.

[2] See Antonio Vilanova's careful presentation of the hypothesis of possible third and fourth cantos in "El peregrino de amor," pp. 421-60.

[3] *Lecciones solemnes*, as cited in Vilanova, "El peregrino de amor," p. 428.

[4] Vilanova, "El peregrino de amor," p. 431.

[5] On the concept of *historia conficta*, see Harry Levin, *The Myth of the Golden Age in the Renaissance* (Bloomington: Indiana University Press, 1969). I cite here Philip Wheelwright's translation of the *Poetics* in his *Aristotle* (New York: Odyssey, 1951).

[6] Argan, *The Europe of the Capitals*, pp. 136-37.

[7] I would like to thank the Indiana University Press for permission to use here Rolfe Humphries' translation of the *Metamorphoses* (Bloomington, 1955). The passages I cite are to be found on pp. 3-16; where I have occasion to refer to the Latin text, I consult the

Loeb edition. On the iconography of the Ages of Metal, see Levin,, pp. 193-99. J. H. Elliott observes: "The idea of an infinite cyclical process, by which all living organisms were subject to growth, maturity and decay, was deeply embedded in European thinking, as was Polybius's application of it to the rise and fall of states. The organic conception of the state in sixteenth-century Europe reinforced the analogy, and history confirmed it. Renaissance historiography had dwelt on the *inclinatio* or the *declinatio* of Rome. If all great empires, including the greatest of them all, had risen only to fall, could Spain alone escape?" ("Self-perception and Decline," p. 48).

[8] Both Alejo Carpentier's *Los pasos perdidos* and Gabriel García Márquez' *Cien años de soledad* represent more or less conscious elaborations of the historico-mythic form Góngora develops in the *Soledades*, and as such they are valid readings of the poem. Carpentier (who borrows his title from the proposition of the *Soledades*) presents his pilgrim as carried backwards in time from the capitalist metropolis (allusively New York or Paris), past the historical strata of the colonial or peripheral metropolis (Caracas-Havana), the town of the interior, the latifundium, the backlands, primitive tribal society, to a genesis landscape of Adam and Eve at the end. *Cien años* goes the way of the pilgrim's anabasis in the first canto, down the river of a century from the initial "soledad confusa" of Macondo's foundation to its apotheosis and destruction in the entry of the Yankee banana company and, of course, the "flood."

[9] Jammes has noted the absence of even a passing reference (excepting the indefinite "templo" of I, 648) to Christian ceremony and dogma in Góngora's presentation of the wedding: "il y a ici une véritable 'paganisation' des cérémonies religieuses catholiques, alors que la tendance générale de cette époque était, au contraire, de 'christianiser' l'héritage culturel du paganisme" (*Etudes*, p. 599, n. 59).

[10] "The Poetic Unity," p. 200. On Góngora's denunciation of seafaring which made the *Soledades* for Jones an "anti-imperialist pastoral," he noted: "The perversion of Nature–*mal nacido pino*–brings only disaster: not merely shipwreck but, as the reference to the Trojan horse shows (I, 374-78), discord and war. Seafaring impelled by greed is not only debased but finally profitless: a moral order is broken together with the physical one and only disaster can follow. . . . Góngora implies that discoveries inspired by greed destroy the discoverers" (*Poems of Góngora*, pp. 26-27). Jammes argues that the theme of greed and navigation in the *Soledades* and elsewhere in Góngora's mature poetry demonstrates a recognition of "le capitalisme naissant et son essor à la fin du Moyen Age" (*Etudes*, p. 603).

[11] *Etudes*, p. 583, n. 22. R. O. Jones observed in the same vein: "The violence in the second *Soledad*, indeed, is great enough to have suggested to some readers that Góngora is preparing a poetic retreat from the idealized life of Nature presented in the first *Soledad*" ("Neoplatonism," p. 4).

[12] To paraphrase Ovid on the question of the relation between the sentimental and the social orders: discord in love leads to kinship discord leads to a loss of natural equality and generosity leads to competition within the community leads to separation into private property and class leads to the organized state leads to mercantile imperialism and war. The pilgrim, to solve the unexpected and potentially dangerous disharmony in the island world, asks the father "que admita yernos los que el trato hijos / litoral hizo, aún antes / que el convecino ardor dulces amantes" (II, 642-44).

[13] The sonnets inspired by Góngora's sickness in 1594 contain the following representation of the Flood:

> Cosas, Celalba mía, he visto extrañas:
> casarse nubes, desbocarse vientos,
> altas torres besar sus fundamentos
> y vomitar la tierra sus entrañas;
>
> duras puentes romper, cual tiernas cañas,
> arroyos prodigiosos, ríos violentos
> mal vadeados de los pensamientos,
> y enfrenados peor de las montañas;
>
> los días de Noé, gentes subidas
> en los más altos pinos levantados,
> en las robustas hayas más crecidas.
>
> Pastores, perros, chozas y ganados
> sobre las aguas ví, sin forma y vidas,
> y nada temí más que mis cuidados. (Millé 261)

The experience described here, I believe, is that of schizophrenia, or (to use Góngora's own term) a "parasismal sueño profundo." Herbert Marcuse notes of the use of psychomimetic drugs (so named because they reproduce schizophrenic states): "The 'trip' involves the dissolution of the ego shaped by established society–an artificial and short-lived dissolution. But the artificial and 'private' liberation anticipates, in a distorted manner, an exigency of social liberation"–*An Essay on Liberation* (Boston: Beacon, 1969), p. 37.

[14] *Esferaimagen*, p. 70. The two friends were the Count of Villamediana and Rodrigo Calderón, Lerma's advisor. After the fall of Lerma's ministry, Calderón was tried and executed for abuses of power and public funds. Villamediana, a skilled poet himself, became a bitter foe of the new *privado*, Olivares. This is probably the reason for his assassination rather than, as the Court gossip accepted by Ticknor had it, that he was having an affair with the Queen. For an interesting discussion of the two deaths and their effect on Góngora, see Edward Churton, *Góngora: An Historical and Critical Essay on the Times of Philip III & IV of Spain* (London: J. Murray, 1862), I, 149-63, 171-77; also Jammes, *Etudes*, pp. 330-34.

[15] On the definition of these two parties, see Jaime Vicens Vives on "Los arbitristas y la economía" in his *Manual de la historia económica de España*, pp. 411-15, and Pierre Vilar on "cuantitativismo" and "bullonismo" in *Crecimiento y desarrollo*, pp. 175-207.

[16] Jammes explains that the "real grandeza" of the figure in the *Soledad segunda* derives from the fact that the Medina Sidonia (like their relatives the Ayamontes and the Duke of Béjar) belonged to the Zúñiga clan which traced its descent to the royal family of Navarre and which was dynastically related to Ferdinand of Aragon. He adds concerning the implications of the portrait: "Il n'est pas interdit de voir dans ces mots un écho des ambitions qu'abritait peut-être la famille des Niebla-Medina Sidonia (et des Ayamonte leurs parents), ambitions qui expliqueraient l'attitude politique de ce clan en 1640" (*Etudes*, p. 281, n. 87).

17 Vilar, *Crecimiento y desarrollo*, p. 448.

18 In his "Two Images in the *Soledades*," p. 784. J. H. Elliott puts the alternative as follows: "Was the reality of Spanish experience to be found in the heroic imperialism of a Charles V or in the humiliating pacifism of a Philip III? In the world of Don Quijote, or in the world of Sancho Panza? Confused at once by its own past and its own present, the Castille of Philip III–the land of the *arbitristas*–sought desperately for an answer" (*Imperial Spain*, p. 316).

Chapter 7: The End of Time

1 *The Hidden God*, trans. Philip Thody (London: Routledge, 1964), p. 376.

2 The portrait of Góngora by Velázquez captures this essential duality. It presents the poet's head in three-quarter profile. The right side of the face is bathed in a flood of golden light which models the high dome of the forehead and extends in a curving line down the long bridge of the nose. The left quarter face is barely visible in shadow. As if Polyphemus, the right eye of the figure stares directly at the spectator. But by looking closely one can also discover the outline of the left eye staring out into (or at) darkness. The zones of light and shadow are mediated in the furrows of the brow between the eyes (the zone of *agudeza*) and along the curve of the mouth, which seems at once cruel and amused. This is the portrait of someone who, like Don Quijote, has been born into an Age of Iron to revive the Age of Gold.

3 *Etudes*, p. 582. Dámaso Alonso: "Continúa Góngora su trabajo, instado y animado por los mismos amigos: logra así añadir 96 versos más, pero al llegar al 936 la labor se atasca; probablemente no sabe qué hacer con aquel extranjero peregrino, ya tan peregrinado. Pasan meses y no añade ni un solo verso; la 'musa,' como él dice por septiembre del 1614, 'está ociosa' " (Góngora, *Obras mayores, I*, 322).

4 There exist, in fact, three different stages of ending in the seventeenth-century texts of the *Soledad segunda* that have come down to us:

(1) The version in Vicuña's *Obras en verso del Homero español* which ends at line 840 ("al viento esgrimirán cuchillo vago") of the hawking scenes.

(2) The version in the manuscript that Pellicer used for his *Lecciones solemnes* which adds the 96 lines Alonso mentions, thus ending at line 936 ("heredado en el último graznido").

(3) The version brought out by Chacón in 1624, apparently with Góngora's consent and collaboration, which has the additional coda describing the end of the hawking and the retirement of the prince and his party along the beach. It is likely that this section was composed as an afterthought ("persuadido por el mismo Don Antonio Chacón," suggested Pellicer) some years after Góngora had abandoned work on the *Soledades*.

On the question of these different endings see Dámaso Alonso's careful study in his Góngora, *Obras mayores, I*, 321-23. He concludes: "Es muy probable que la *Segunda Soledad* se fuera haciendo a retazos, y corrigiéndose a retazos también; por lo menos así ocurrió con la última parte" (pp. 351-52, n. 30).

[5] As cited by Espinosa Medrano, who countered: "Esso imperfecto, esso por acabar, que se dexó Góngora, es mucho mejor, que lo muy concluido, y sellado de los otros"– *Apologético en favor de Don Luis de Góngora, Revue Hispanique*, 65 (1925), pp. 498-99, 501.

[6] On the effects of Lerma's fall on Góngora's poetic and political career, see Jammes, *Etudes*, pp. 585-86; E. Orozco Díaz' rather sketchy "Espiritu y vida en la creación de las *Soledades* gongorinas," *Papeles de Son Armadans*, 87 (1963), 226-52; and Joaquín de Entrambasaguas, *Estudios y ensayos sobre Góngora y el barroco* (Madrid: Editora Nacional, 1975), pp. 151-75.

[7] *Etudes*, p. 306. Jammes adds that the portrait corresponds on a political level to "l'idéal esthétique, moral et social qui s'était déjà exprimé dans les *Solitudes*."

[8] The classic case of the enigmatic ending in the *romance lírico* is the "Romance del Infante Arnaldos" which Menéndez Pidal used to illustrate the fragmentation of medieval epic and quasi epic. Góngora is certainly not alone among the Spanish Baroque poets in his recourse to the device. What is peculiar to it here, however, is its ethical and political resonance. R. O. Jones explained: "*Si puede*: but it cannot: Orlando will lay all waste. Góngora introduces thus, with the skill of genius, a quiet comment on the precariousness of human happiness. But the poem is not, after all, entirely a pessimistic one: if Góngora expects us to know from Ariosto the antecedents of the action he must equally expect us to remember the sequel: Angelica and Medoro will reign happily in Cathay, where Orlando cannot reach them. Furthermore, Orlando can hurt but cannot destroy Nature. What, after all, is transitory is Count Orlando and his kind. The poem, with its quiet allusion to what is to come, is 'open-ended' and invites the reader to glance down the vistas it opens" (*Poems of Góngora*, p. 20).

[9] The guide who ferries Andrenio and Critilo across the Lake of Ink to the Island of Immortality is named, in a tacit homage to the *persona* of the *Soledades*, El Peregrino. The Baroque conceit of the identity of ends and beginnings is neatly expressed in Calderón's sonnet on the roses which "cuna y sepulcro en un botón hallaron." The force of disillusion such devices and images carry is not only metaphysical but also historical. They are products of an age when both the genesis and the decadence of Spain's empire were simultaneously visible. Cf. Quevedo in his "Salmo XVII": "Miré los muros de la patria mía, / si un tiempo fuertes, ya desmoronados."

[10] Joaquín Casalduero, *Sentido y forma de "Los trabajos de Persiles y Sigismunda"* (Buenos Aires: Editorial Sudamericana, 1947), pp. 19-20.

[11] Pedro Espinosa, cited previously in support of the "Andalusianism" of this passage, wrote of the young aristocrat: "Cuando más se debía a los ojos y voluntades de la Corte . . . , cuando su suegro el de Lerma mandaba el mundo, sordo a sus ruegos y promesas, trató de retirarse a la soledad de Huelva, diciéndole: 'Tanto harta, señor, una fuente como un río. La Corte, donde toda vida es corta, quiero lejos, como pintura del Greco; si bien no tanto que enfríe mas ni tan cerca que abrase' " (*Elogio al Retrato*, in Espinosa, *Obras*, p. 251). We may compare this attitude with that expressed by the pilgrim in the "Bienaventurado albergue" encomium or by Góngora in his youthful *letrilla* "Andeme yo caliente" (1581):

> Traten otros del gobierno
> del mundo y sus monarquías,

mientras gobiernan mis días
mantequillas y pan tierno,
y las mañanas de invierno
naranjada y aguardiente,
y ríase la gente.

12 "Two Images," p. 781. Góngora's several poems on the deaths of Rodrigo Calderón (by execution) and Villamediana (by assassination) are built around the image of a knife or axe–which suggests the "fatal acero" of the hawking, or the "filos de homicida hierro" (II, 159) the pilgrim fears in his soliloquy. See, for example, Millé 251 where Calderón appears as "Fénix en la muerte si en la vida / ave" and "desvanecida pluma." (As I noted earlier, Calderón was convicted of extortion.)

13 ". . . le hasard qui crée la nécessité, illusion de l'homme–ce morceau de nature devenu fou–la nécessité créant le hasard comme ce qui la limite et la définit *a contrario*, la nécessité niant le hasard 'pied à pied' dans le vers, le hasard niant à son tour la nécessité puisque le *full-employment* des mots est impossible et la nécessité abolissant à son tour le hasard par le suicide du Poème et de la poésie"–Jean-Paul Sartre, "Préface," *Poésies*, by Stéphane Mallarmé (Paris: Gallimard, 1967). Cf. Góngora:

Pasos de un peregrino son errante
cuantos me dictó versos dulce musa:
en soledad confusa
perdidos unos, otros inspirados.

"Verse can only weave a garland of freedom round something that has already been liberated from all fetters. If the author's action consists in disclosing buried meaning, if his heroes must first break out of their prisons and, in desperate struggles or long, wearisome wanderings, attain the home of their dreams–their freedom from terrestrial gravity–then the power of verse, which can spread a carpet of flowers over the chasm, is not sufficient to build a practicable road across it"–Georg Lukács, *The Theory of the Novel*, trans. Anna Bostock (Cambridge: M.I.T. Press, 1971), p. 58. "For language is in every case not only communication of the communicable but also, at the same time, a symbol of the noncommunicable"–Walter Benjamin, "On Language as Such and on the Languages of Man," in *Reflections*, trans. Edmund Jephcott (New York: Harcourt, Brace, Jovanovich, 1978), p. 331.

Bibliography

Major Texts of the *Soledades* (listed in historical order by editor)

Chacón, Antonio. Manuscrito Chacón (c. 1624). Reproduced by Raymond Foulché-Delbosc in *Obras poéticas de Don Luis de Góngora*, II. New York: Hispanic Society of America, 1921 and 1970. Original in the Biblioteca Nacional of Madrid.

López de Vicuña, Juan. *Obras en verso del Homero español*. Madrid: Viuda de L. Sánchez, 1627. Facsimile prepared by Dámaso Alonso. Madrid: C.S.I.C., 1963.

Pellicer de Salas y Tovar, José. *Lecciones solemnes a las obras de Don Luis de Góngora y Argote*. Madrid: Imprenta del Reino, 1630. Facsimile. Hildesheim and New York: Georg Olms Verlag, 1971.

Hoces y Córdoba, Gonzalo. *Todas las obras de Don Luis de Góngora en varios poemas*. Madrid: Imprenta del Reino, 1633. Often republished during the seventeenth century.

Salcedo Coronel, José García de. *Las "Soledades" de Don Luis de Góngora comentadas*. Madrid: Imprenta Real, 1636.

Castro, Adolfo de. In Biblioteca de Autores Españoles XXXII, *Poesía lírica*. Madrid: Rivadeneyra, 1854.

Alonso, Dámaso. Góngora, *Las Soledades*. Madrid: Revista de Occidente, 1927.
(a) Madrid: Ediciones del Arbol, 1935. (With the full title Góngora, *Obras mayores, I, Las Soledades*.)
(b) Madrid: Cruz y Raya, 1936.
(c) Madrid: Sociedad de Estudios y Publicaciones, 1956.
(Editions a, b, and c above have Alonso's reconstruction of the "primitive" text.)

Millé y Giménez, Isabel and Juan. Góngora, *Obras completas*. 1943; Madrid: Aguilar, 1961.

Beverley, John. Góngora, *Soledades*. Madrid: Cátedra, 1979.

. . .

Alonso, Dámaso. *La lengua poética de Góngora*. 1935; Madrid: C.S.I.C., 1961.

______. *Estudios y ensayos gongorinos*. Madrid: Gredos, 1960.

———. *Góngora y el "Polifemo."* 5th ed. Madrid: Gredos, 1967.

Ares Montes, José. "Del otoño del gongorismo." *Revista de Filología Española*, 44 (1961), 283-322.

Argan, G. Carlo. *The Europe of the Capitals: 1600-1700.* Geneva: Skira, 1964.

Artigas, Miguel. *Don Luis de Góngora y Argote: Biografía y estudio crítico.* Madrid: Revista de Archivos, 1925.

Bennassar, Bartolomé. *Valladolid au siècle d'or, une ville de Castille et sa campagne au XVIe siècle.* Paris and The Hague: Mouton, 1967.

Benjamin, Walter. *The Origins of German Tragic Drama.* English trans. London: New Left Books, 1974.

———. *Reflections.* Trans. Edmund Jephcott. New York: Harcourt, Brace, Jovanovich, 1978.

Beverley, John. "*Soledad primera*, lines 1-61." *Modern Language Notes*, 88 (1973), 233-48.

———. "The Language of Contradiction: Aspects of Góngora's *Soledades*." *Ideologies and Literature*, 1, No. 5 (1978), 28-56.

———. "Confusion and Construction in the *Soledades*." *Dispositio (Revista Hispánica de Semiótica Literaria)*, 3, No. 9 (1978), forthcoming.

Borah, Woodrow. *New Spain's Century of Depression.* Berkeley: University of California Press, 1951.

Carilla, Emilio. "Trayectoria del gongorismo en Hispanoamérica." *Atenea*, 142 (1961), 110-21.

Carillo y Sotomayor, Luis. *Libro de la erudición poética* (1611). Facsimile ed. Madrid: C.S.I.C., 1946.

Casalduero, Joaquín. *Sentido y forma de "Los trabajos de Persiles y Sigismunda."* Buenos Aires: Editorial Sudamericana, 1947.

Cascales, Francisco. *Cartas filológicas.* Vol. 1. Clásicos Castellanos. Madrid: Espasa-Calpe, 1930.

Castro, Américo. *Hacia Cervantes.* Madrid: Taurus, 1967.

Caudwell, Christopher. *Illusion and Reality: A Study in the Sources of Poetry.* New York: International, 1967.

Chomsky, Noam. *Cartesian Linguistics.* New York: Harper, 1966.

———. *Language and Mind.* New York: Harcourt, Brace & World, 1968.

Churton, Edward. *Góngora: An Historical and Critical Essay on the Times of Philip III and IV of Spain.* 2 vol. London: J. Murray, 1862.

Collard, Andrée. *Nueva poesía: conceptismo, culteranismo en la crítica española.* Madrid: Castalia, 1967.

Córdoba, Francisco de (Abad de Rute). *Examen del "Antídoto" o apología por las "Soledades"* (c. 1615). Text in Artigas.

Crawford, J. P. Wickersham. "The Setting of Góngora's *Las Soledades.*" *Hispanic Review*, 3 (1939), 347-49.

Cunningham, Gilbert. *The "Solitudes" of Luis de Góngora.* Baltimore: Johns Hopkins University Press, 1968.

Díaz de Rivas, Pedro. *Discursos apologéticos por el estylo del "Poliphemo" y "Soledades"* (c. 1615). Text in Gates.

Dubois, Claude-Gilbert. *Mythe et langage au seizième siècle.* Bordeaux: Ducros, 1970.

Elliott, J. H. *Imperial Spain: 1469-1716.* New York: New American Library, 1966.

_____. "Self-perception and Decline in Early Seventeenth-Century Spain." *Past and Present*, 74 (1977), 41-61.

Empson, William. *Some Versions of the Pastoral.* Norfolk, Conn.: New Directions, 1961.

Entrambasaguas, Joaquín de. *Estudios y ensayos sobre Góngora y el barroco.* Madrid: Editora Nacional, 1975.

Espinosa, Pedro. *Obras de Pedro Espinosa.* Ed. Francisco Rodríguez Marín. Madrid: Real Academia Española, 1909.

Espinosa Medrano, Juan de. *Apologético en favor de Don Luis de Góngora* (c. 1662). Ed. Ventura García Calderón. *Revue Hispanique*, 65 (1925).

Foucault, Michel. *Les mots et les choses; une archéologie des sciences humaines.* Paris: Gallimard, 1966.

_____. *Madness and Civilization.* Trans. Richard Howard. New York: New American Library, 1967.

Gaos, Vicente. *Temas y problemas de la literatura española.* Madrid: Guadarrama, 1959.

García Lorca, Federico. *Obras completas.* Madrid: Aguilar, 1966.

Gates, Eunice Joiner, ed. *Documentos gongorinos.* México: Colegio de México, 1960.

Genette, Gérard. *Figures.* Paris: Seuil, 1966.

_____. *Figures II.* Paris: Seuil, 1969.

Geske, Rudolf. *Góngoras Warnrede im Zeichen der Hekate.* Berlin: Colloquium Verlag, 1964.

Glendinning, Nigel. "La fortuna de Góngora en el siglo XVIII." *Revista de Filología Española*, 44 (1961), 323-49.

Goig, Cedomil. "Góngora y la retórica manierista de la dificultad docta." *Atenea*, 142 (1961), 168-78.

Goldmann, Lucien. *The Hidden God.* Trans. Philip Thody. London: Routledge, 1964.

Góngora y Argote, Luis de. See listings under Major Texts of the *Soledades*.

González de Cellorigo, Martín. *Memorial de la política necesaria y útil restauración de la república de España.* Valladolid, 1600.

Gracián, Baltasar. *Obras completas.* Madrid: Aguilar, 1960.

Guillén, Claudio. *Literature as System.* Princeton: Princeton University Press, 1971.

Hart, Thomas. "The Pilgrim's Role in the First *Solitude*." *Modern Language Notes*, 92 (1977), 213-26.

Hatzfeld, Helmut. *Estudios sobre el barroco.* Madrid: Gredos, 1964.

Hobsbawm, Eric. "The General Crisis of the European Economy in the Seventeenth Century." *Past and Present*, 5 and 6 (1954), 33-53, 44-65.

Jameson, Fred. *Marxism and Form.* Princeton: Princeton University Press, 1971.

Jammes, Robert. *Etudes sur l'oeuvre poétique de Don Luis de Góngora.* Bordeaux: Féret et Fils, 1967.

Jáuregui, Juan de. *Antídoto a la pestilente poesía de las "Soledades"* (1614). Text in Gates.

Jones, Royston O. "The Poetic Unity of the *Soledades* of Góngora." *Bulletin of Hispanic Studies*, 31 (1954), 189-204.

_____. "Neoplatonism and the *Soledades*." *Bulletin of Hispanic Studies*, 40 (1963), 1-16.

_____. "Góngora and Neoplatonism Again." *Bulletin of Hispanic Studies*, 43 (1966), 117-20.

_____. *Poems of Góngora.* Cambridge: The University Press, 1966.

_____. "Poets and Peasants." In *Homenaje a William L. Fichter.* Ed. A. David Kossoff and José Amor y Vásquez. Madrid: Castalia, 1971.

Lezama Lima, José. *Esferaimagen.* Barcelona: Turquets, 1970.

Levin, Harry. *The Myth of the Golden Age in the Renaissance*. Bloomington: Indiana University Press, 1969.

Lida de Malkiel, María Rosa. "El hilo narrativo de las *Soledades*." *Boletín de la Academia Argentina de Letras*, 26 (1961), 349-59.

_____. *La tradición clásica en España*. Barcelona: Ariel, 1975.

Lukács, Georg. *The Theory of the Novel*. Trans. Anna Bostock. Cambridge: M.I.T. Press, 1971.

Macrí, Oreste. *Fernando de Herrera*. Madrid: Gredos, 1959.

Maravall, José Antonio. *Teatro y literatura en la sociedad barroca*. Madrid: Seminarios y Ediciones, 1972.

_____. *La cultura del barroco*. Barcelona: Ariel, 1975.

Marcuse, Herbert. *An Essay on Liberation*. Boston: Beacon, 1969.

_____. *The Aesthetic Dimension*. Boston: Beacon, 1978.

Marx, Karl. *A Contribution to the Critique of Political Economy*. Ed. Maurice Dobb. Moscow: Progress, 1970.

_____. *Capital*. Vol I. Moscow: Foreign Languages, 1961.

_____. *Grundrisse*. Ed. Martin Nicolaus. New York: Vintage, 1963.

Merrington, John. "Town and Country in the Transition to Capitalism." In *The Transition from Feudalism to Capitalism*. Ed. Rodney Hilton. London: New Left Books, 1976.

Molho, Maurice. *Sémantique et poétique: à propos des "Solitudes" de Góngora*. Bordeaux: Ducros, 1969.

Mumford, Lewis. *The Culture of the Cities*. New York: Harcourt, 1938.

Muñoz G., L. "Estructura de las *Soledades*." *Atenea*, 142 (1961), 179-201.

Nuñez de Reinoso, Alonso. *Historia de los amores de Clareo y Florisea, y de los trabajos de Isea* (1552). Text in Biblioteca de Autores Españoles III, *Novelistas anteriores a Cervantes*. Madrid: Atlas, 1963.

Orozco Díaz, Emilio. "Espíritu y vida en la creación de las *Soledades* gongorinas." *Papeles de Son Armadans*, 87 (1963), 226-52.

_____. *Lope y Góngora frente a frente*. Madrid: Gredos, 1973.

Ovid, *Metamorphoses*. Trans. Rolfe Humphries. Bloomington: Indiana University Press, 1955.

Pabst, Walter. *La creación gongorina en los poemas "Polifemo" y "Soledades."* Trans. Nicolás Marín. Madrid: C.S.I.C., 1966.

Panofsky, Erwin. *Idea: A Concept in Art Theory*. Columbia: University of South Carolina Press, 1968.

Parker, Alexander A. *Polyphemus and Galatea: A Study in the Interpretation of a Baroque Poem*. Austin: University of Texas Press; Edinburgh: University of Edinburgh Press, 1977.

Pellicer, José. See listing under Major Texts of the *Soledades*.

Poggioli, Renato. *The Oaten Flute: Essays on Pastoral Poetry and the Pastoral Ideal*. Cambridge: Harvard University Press, 1975.

Reyes, Alfonso. *Cuestiones gongorinas*. Madrid: Espasa-Calpe, 1927.

Rivers, Elias. "El conceptismo del *Polifemo*." *Atenea*, 142 (1961), 102-09.

_____. "The Pastoral Paradox of Natural Arts." *Modern Language Notes*, 77 (1962), 144-50.

Salcedo Coronel, José García de. See listing under Major Texts of the *Soledades*.

Salinas, Pedro. *Ensayos de literatura hispánica*. Madrid: Aguilar, 1968.

Salomon, Noël. *La campagne de Nouvelle Castille à la fin du XVIe siècle*. Paris: S.E.V.P.E.N., 1964.

_____. *Recherches sur le thème paysan dans la "comedia" au temps de Lope de Vega*. Bordeaux: Féret et Fils, 1967.

Sartre, Jean-Paul. "Préface." *Poésies*. By Stéphane Mallarmé. Paris: Gallimard, 1967.

Smith, C. Colin. "On the Use of Spanish Theoretical Works in the Debate on Gongorism." *Bulletin of Hispanic Studies*, 39 (1962), 165-76.

_____. "An Approach to Góngora's *Polifemo*." *Bulletin of Hispanic Studies*, 42 (1965), 217-38.

Spitzer, Leo. "Zu Góngoras *Soledades*." *Volkstum und Kultur der Romanen*, 2 (1929), 240-60.

_____. "La *Soledad primera* de Góngora: notas críticas y explicativas a la nueva edición de Dámaso Alonso." *Revista de Filología Hispánica*, 2 (1940), 151-76.

_____. Note, in "Revista de Revistas." *Revista de Filología Hispánica*, 2 (1940), 85.

Valencia, Pedro de. "Carta a Don Luis de Góngora en censura de sus poesías" (1613). Two versions in Millé y Giménez (eds.), Góngora, *Obras completas*, "Epistolario." Madrid: Aguilar, 1961.

Vicens Vives, Jaime. *Manual de historia económica de España.* 4th ed. Barcelona: Editorial Vicens-Vives, 1965.

Vilanova, Antonio. "El peregrino de amor en las *Soledades* de Góngora." In *Estudios dedicados a Menéndez Pidal.* Vol III. Madrid: C.S.I.C., 1952, 421-60.

_____. "Preceptistas españoles de los siglos XVI y XVII." In *Historia general de las literaturas hispánicas.* Ed. Guillermo Díaz-Plaja. Vol. III. Madrid: Editorial Barna, 1953, 281-580.

_____. *Las fuentes y los temas del "Polifemo" de Góngora.* Madrid: C.S.I.C., 1957. Vol. I.

Vilar, Pierre. "El problema de la formación del capitalismo," and "El tiempo del *Quijote.*" In *Crecimiento y desarrollo: reflexiones sobre el caso expañol.* Spanish trans. Barcelona: Ariel, 1964.

Vossler, Kurt. *La soledad en la poesía española.* Madrid: Revista de Occidente, 1941.

_____. *La poesía de la soledad en España.* Spanish trans. Ramón de la Serna. Buenos Aires: Losada, 1946.

Waley, Pamela. "Some Uses of Classical Mythology in the *Soledades* of Góngora." *Bulletin of Hispanic Studies,* 36 (1959), 193-209.

Wardropper, Bruce. "The Complexity of the Simple in Góngora's *Soledad primera.*" *The Journal of Medieval and Renaissance Studies,* 7 (1977), 35-51.

Wheelwright, Philip. *Aristotle.* New York: Odyssey, 1951.

Williams, Raymond. *The Country and the City.* New York: Oxford University Press, 1975.

Wilson, Edward M. *The "Solitudes" of Don Luis de Góngora.* Cambridge: The University Press, 1965.

Woodward, L. J. "Two Images in the *Soledades* of Góngora." *Modern Language Notes,* 76 (1961), 773-85.

In the PURDUE UNIVERSITY MONOGRAPHS IN ROMANCE LANGUAGES series the following monographs have been published thus far:

1. *John R. Beverley:* Aspects of Gongóra's "Soledades".
Amsterdam, 1980. iv, 139 pp. Bound.

2. *Robert Francis Cook:* "Chanson d'Antioche", Chanson de geste: Le cycle de la croisade est il épique?
Amsterdam, 1980. vi, 107 pp. Bound.

3. *Sandy Petrey:* History in the Text: "Quatrevingt-Treize" and the French Revolution.
Amsterdam, 1980. viii, 129 pp. Bound.

4. *Walter Kasell:* Marcel Proust and the Strategy of Reading.
Amsterdam, 1980. x, 125 pp. Bound.

5. *Inés Azar:* Discurso retórico y mundo pastoral en la 'Egloga segunda' de Garcilaso.
Amsterdam, 1980/81. ca. 160 pp. Bound.

6. *Roy Armes:* The Films of Alain Robbe-Grillet
Amsterdam, 1980/81. ca. 220 pp. Bound.